AF541055

DIMENSIONS OF POPULATION GROWTH

DIMENSIONS OF POPULATION GROWTH

Edited by

R.N. MISRA

ANMOL PUBLICATIONS PVT. LTD.
NEW DELHI - 110 002 (INDIA)

ANMOL PUBLICATIONS PVT. LTD.
4374/4B, Ansari Road, Daryaganj
New Delhi - 110 002
Ph.: 23261597, 23278000
Visit us: www.anmolpublications.com

Dimensions of Population Growth

First Edition, 2003

ISBN 81-261-1539-4

PRINTED IN INDIA

Published by J.L. Kumar for Anmol Publications Pvt. Ltd., New Delhi - 110 002 and Printed at Tarun Offset Printers, (Delhi)

Contents

Foreword

Population explosion is a burning problem of our country. India occupies second place in the world in population whereas occupies 7th place in terms of area. India has 2.4 per cent of world's land with 16 per cent of world's population. The nature has given us air, land and all other resources with limited means. Unless a positive and effective check has been made on the growth of population, no doubt India will overtake China and we will face a number of problems like food, unemployment, health and what not?. Again the survival of a man is a big question after 2025. It is high-time for us, unless some bold steps are not to be taken it is very difficult for our country to face this alarming situation. So, government, different NGO's, political parties and public as a whole should have to think seriously and steps have to be taken to solve these problems.

This book is of great importance to the government, planners, research scholars, non-government organisations and others who are seriously thinking for the economic development of our country as a whole.

Dr. R.P. Sarma

Prof. of Economics (Rtd)

Acknowledgements

I am very much thankful to all paper contributors of this book and mostly to Dr. R.P. Sarma, Prof of Economics for his help and cooperation to edit this book. I am also thankful to my friend Sri Subash Chandra Padhy, Lecturer in English for his kind help and timely cooperation in editing this book.

Again my thanks go to my wife Smt. Svarana Prava who has helped me all the times, whenever I needed her help. Her co-operation in right time has inspired me to edit this book. My heartful thanks to my two beloved sons Roopesh Kumar and Rookesh Kumar who helped me all the times and their kind affection and love encouraged me to edit this book.

I am very much thankful and grateful to Sri Kripal D. Joshi of Anmol Publications (P) Ltd., New Delhi, who has already accepted my proposal in publishing this book in spite of his busy schedule in the beginning of the session. Again I on behalf of all paper writers thank him for his kind cooperation. I also thank all the staff, technical personnel and others of Anmol Publications (P) Ltd. for their kind cooperation shown to me in publishing the book at short span of time.

R.N. Misra

The Contributors

Sri G. Rajgopal Rao (b. 1951), joined as a lecturer in commerce in 1975. Mr. Rao has published two books and eight articles in different journals. He has submitted his Ph.D thesis in Berhampur University in the month of July, 2002. Now he is working at Govt. College, Bhawanipatna, Dist. Kalahandi, Orissa as a Senior Reader in Commerce.

Sri Baidyanath Dali (b. 1959), joined as a lecturer in commerce in the year 1983. He has published 10 articles in different journals. He has submitted his Ph.D thesis in Berhampur University since April 2002. At present he is working at Govt. Science College, Chatrapur, Orissa as a Senior Lecturer in Commerce.

Mr. D.Tata Rao (b. 196l), passed M.Com, from Andhra University in 1983, B.Ed in 1987, and M.Ed in 1990. He has published five articles and currently purjuing his Ph.D. Now he is working as a Senior Lecturer in Govt. Degree College, Ichhapuram, Andhra University, A.P.

Sri Debadatta Choudhary is a Senior Reader in Economics, working at B.P. Mahavidylaya, Sauntiapalli, Dist. Ganjam, Berhampur University. He has published a number of articles in different journals. He is also associated with a number of voluntary associations.

Dr. Suresh Ku. Sahu, is a Reader and Head, Dept. of Economics, Science College, Hinjilicut, Orissa. Dr. Sahu has a number of publications. He is also guiding two lecturers for doctoral research.

Dr. Nirmal Chandra Das, Reader in Anthropology. Now he is working at D.D.College, Keonjhar, Sambalpur University, Orissa. He has a lot of publication work to his credit.

Dr.(Smt.) Nakshetra Mala Panigrahy, M.S.O., F.I.C.OG, FIMCH, Professor and Head, Dept. of Obst & Gynaecology (Rtd) M.K.C.G Medical College, Hospital, Berhampur. Dr. Panigrahy has published many articles in different journals. She is now associated with number of voluntary organisations and Chief Consultant of Bansadhara Hospital, Berhampur, Orissa.

Mr. R.N. Dalai, a Senior Lecturer in Economics working at Khallikote (Auto) College, Berhampur. He has published five articles. He is associated with a number of voluntary organisations.

Mr. Nilamadhaba Mohanty, did his M.A in Economics from Berhampur University and joined as a research scholar at Economics Dept. of Berhampur University.

Mr. Santosh Kumar Pradhan (b. 1975), did his M.A. in Economics in 1997. He has published four articles and doing his Ph.D. on Problem of Child Labour. His five Oriya Drama books are ready to publish. He is associated with a number of voluntary organisations.

Sri R. L. Panigrahy, (b. 1975), did his M.A in Economics, PGDCA, Post Graduate Diploma in Personal Management and Industrial Relations. Mr Panigrahy has published five books and two books are in the press. He has published 12 articles in different journals. He is working as a Faculty Member in Computer in the Dept. of Commerce, Science College, Hinjilicut. He is associated with a number of voluntary organisations.

Prof. (Dr.) R.P. Sarma, a retired Professor of Economics of

Berhampur University. He retired from his service in the year 1996. He has produced eight Ph.D. scholars and at present he is the Director, Institute of Economic Studies, Berhampur. He is also associated with a number of organisations.

Dr. S.N. Tripathy, (b. 1957) is a renowned researcher and author of more than 10 books. He has completed many projects funded by ICSSR and UGC. He has produced three Ph.D. scholars and at present guiding more than five scholars. Presently he is associated with Dept. of Economics, Aska Science College, Orissa.

Mr. Premananda Pradhan completed his Post-graduate from Berhampur University in the year 1997. He has published more than eight articles and is also author of a book titled *Girl Child in India*. At present he is pursuing Ph.D. at the Dept. of Economics in Berhampur University.

Mr. Roopesh Ku. Misra (b. 1974), did his B.Sc., LL.B., from Berhampur University. He has also done his MBA from NIHRD, Madras. He has also done PGDCA and CIC programme on Computer. An MCA from IGNOU, currently he is working at HDFC Bank, New Delhi. He has published more than 10 articles at different journals.

Dr. Prakash Ch. Misra, Senior Reader, Dept. of Commerce, Berhampur University, Orissa. He has produced more than five Ph.D. scholars and at present guiding 8 Ph.D. scholars. He is also author of more than three books and published more than 30 articles at different journals.

1
Population and Economics Growth

—*Prof. R.P. Sarma*

It was Thomas Malthus at the end of 18th century for the first time realized the importance of growth of population for the development of a country. He linked population to production of foodgrains the main activity of economy at that period. Of course his thesis that the population grow at the geometrical proportions against the growth of foodgrains in arithmetic progression as the crisis in the economy is not accepted today, but the fact remains that the growth of population influences the growth and development of an economy. This was his main intention in propounding his population thesis which is an accepted fact today.

The population statistics regarded as an important aspect of an economy to know the people and their problems. Population census started computation in the middle of the 19th century. By the end of 19th century the world population estimated at about 100 crores. In the 20th century census is being taken at every ten .years in India from 1901 onwards. At the beginning of the 20th century India has a population of about 24 crores and in the first

50 years of the century it increased to 36 crores which at the end of the century in 2001 reached at about 103 crores. India is the second largest populated country in the world after China with a population of 128 crores. The world has total population of about 606 crores by the year 2000, of which 10 largest populated countries have about 59 per cent population, which includes 6 countries of Asia. China and India together constitute about 38 per cent of the world population.

Growth of Population in India

In the first decade after Independence, in nineteen fifties, the annual rate of growth of population suddenly jumped to 2.16 per cent from that of 1.33 per cent in 1941-51 decade. In sixties the growth of population was highest with 2.5 per cent per annum. India was the first country to take officially to check population growth by resorting to preventive measures. The first clinic to advice the couples about the methods of family planning was started in Karnataka, the erstwhile state of Mysore was the pioneer in the field of family planning when there were no such efforts in the western countries.

Growth of Population in Orissa

In the first half the 20th century the growth of population was comparatively slow in India, but it was accelerated in the second half. In Orissa too the growth trend of population followed the national trend but remained lower to the national growth ratio. In the first half of the 20th century Indian growth rate of population on an average remained 2.0 per cent while in the second half it remained 2.22 per cent. In the same period Orissa's growth rate of population in the first half remained at 1.68 per cent while in the second half it increased to 1.91 per

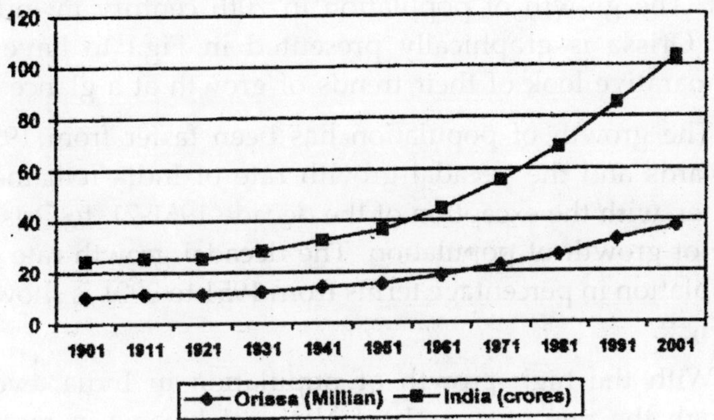

Fig.1 Growth of Population in 20th Century

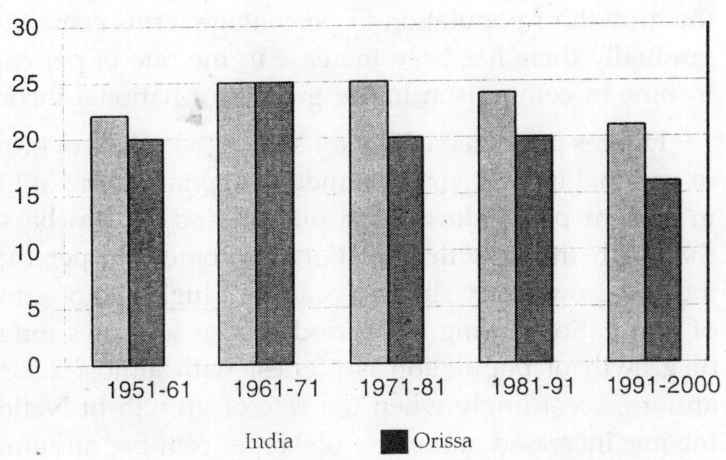

Fig.2 Growth of Population in Percentage Terms

cent. The growth of population in 20th century in India and Orissa is graphically presented in Fig.l to have a comparative look of their trends of growth at a glance.

The growth of population has been faster from 1951 onwards and the decadal growth rate of India remained higher, with the exception of the decade 1961-71, to Orissa rate of growth of population. The decadal growth rate of population in percentage terms from 1951 to 2001 is shown in Fig.2.

With the high growth of population in India, even though the rate of growth of National Income in recent years has been in the increasing trend the per capita income of the people has been in the declining trend. The high rate of growth of population depresses the real economic growth in our country, which is one of the important obstacles of economic growth among others. During the first plan period, 1951-56, there was 1.5 per cent growth of the national income but the per capita income of the people of India shows negative of -0.4 per cent in current prices. With the growth of population in percentage terms came down gradually there has been increase in the rate of per capita income in comparison to the growth of national income.

Figures presented in Table 1 shows the trends of growth of national income vis-a-vis the per capita income of India in current prices during the plan period.. It can be seen that with the growth of national income, the per capita income grown very slowly because of high rate of growth of population during the period. In the seventies the rate of growth of population is highest with almost 2.50 per annum, accordingly when the rate of growth of National Income increased at the rate of 3.5 per cent per annum the per capita income showed very meagre growth rate annually, in some years it was negative which is not shown in the table as the figures show the five year average growth rates.

Table 1

Growth Rates of National Income and per capita Income of India (At Current prices)

Year	*National Income*	*Per Capita Income*
First Plan 1951-56	1.5	-0.4
Second Plan 1958-61	9.4	7.3
Third Plan 1961-66	4.1	1.7
Fourth Plan 1969-74	11.0	8.5
Fifth Plan 1974-79	10.4	7.9
Sixth Plan 1980-85	15.1	12.6
Seventh Plan 1985-90	14.1	11.7
Eighth Plan 1992-97	16.2	14.0
Ninth Plan 1997-2002 (1997-01)	13.35	10.52

Source: Economic Survey, India 1999-2000 and Economic Survey, Orissa, 2001-2002.

In Orissa the annual growth rate of population slowed down from 2.50 in 1971 to 1.59 in 2001, accordingly it can be observe from Table 2 that the per capita income of the state increased higher as the rate of growth of population decreased. All the figures in the Table are in current prices hence the growth rates are at the higher percentage level. This shows that the growth of population or the slowing down of the rate of growth of population has influenced the per capita income of the state. In the constant 1993-94 prices the growth of state income and the per capita income between the years 1993-94 and 2000-01 on an average annually comes to 7.47 and 4.74 per cent respectively.

Table 2

Growth of State Income and Population

Year	*State Income Rs .in Crores*	*Per Capita Income Rs.*	*Annual Growth Rate of Population Per cent*
1965-66	640	329	
1970-71	1083 (13.85)	499 (10.33)	2.50
1980-81	3225 (19.77)	1101 (12.06)	2.01
1990-91	9664 (19.96)	3027 (17.49)	2.00
2000-01	30795 (21.86)	8547 (18.23)	1.59

Note: Figures in parentheses indicate annual growth rate in per cent.

The trends of the growth of these two incomes are shown in Table 3. It can be seen that the per capita income moved rapidly downwards in comparison to the state income even though there is slowing down of population growth in the state. The figures indicate that the slow growth of population in Orissa has not influenced the increase in the per capita income of the state. There are other factors which depressed the growth rate of per capita income.

Urbanisation in Orissa

Urbanisation is regarded as one of the factors that boost the economic development of a region. Urbanisation and urban population is also comparatively low in Orissa. The state has eight cities with a population of one lakh and more. The percentage of urban population is now 14.97 (2001 Census), which is lowest among Indian states with the exception of Assam and Bihar. Of course the urban population in Orissa grown rapidly, from mere 4 per cent in 1951 to about 15 per cent in a period of fifty years by 2001, it is not equivalent to the Indian percentage of urban population of 27.78 per cent. Tamil Nadu has the highest percentage of urban population in India which is 43.86 per cent.

Table 3

State Income and per capita Income of Orissa in Constant 1993-94 Prices

Year	*State Income Rs. 1000 Crores*	*Per cent of Growth*	*Per capita Income Rs.*	*Per cent of Growth*
1993-94	6859	—	7698	—
1994-95	7343	7.49	8088	5.06
1995-96	7878	6.85	8498	5.06
1996-97	8521	8.86	9036	6.33
1997-98	8907	4.53	9288	5.99
1998-99	9489	6.53	9733	4.79
1999-00	10077	6.20	10067	3.44
2000-01	10449	4.19	10254	2.52

Source: Economic Survey, Orissa, 2001-2002, Bhubaneswar.

Rate of Literacy

Literacy is another important factor which influences economic growth through the development of human resources. In literacy also Orissa is at the lowest ladder in the national scenario. According to the census of 2001 Orissa has now 63.61 per cent literacy which is higher only to the four states of Andhra Pradesh, Rajasthan, Uttar Pradesh and Bihar. It is about 2 per cent lower to the percentage of literacy of the country. But in the male literacy of 75.85 per cent is almost equal to the Indian figure. Even though the male rate of literacy is more than 85 per cent in seven of the coastal districts of Orissa, most of the pockets of the tribal districts have very low rate of literacy going down to 41.21 per cent (district of Malkangiri). Female literacy is 50.97 per cent in the state, but it has not exceeded 71 per cent in any of the districts of Orissa. The two Southern districts of Malkangiri and Nabarangpur have the lowest literacy of about 21 per cent among the female population.

Most Backward State

Even after 50 years of planned development in the state, by the turn of the century Orissa still remains as the most backward state in India. The recent figures of population below the poverty line and the per capita income of the people of the state clearly indicate it. Orissa has the highest people below the poverty line of 47.2 per cent, as per the norms of poverty line determined by the Planning Commission even the state of Bihar is below it. The per capita income of the state is Rs. 8,733 according to the prices of 2001 shows that it is again the lowest in India. Punjab has highest per capita income of Rs. 23.040 and accordingly the lowest number of people below poverty line of only 6.2 per cent.

Table 4 provides the figures of per capita income and percentage of population below the poverty line of the major states of India.

Conclusion

High growth of population is certainly hindrance to the economic development of a region, but it alone cannot be taken as the sole factor for the underdevelopment of a state. In Orissa even though the rate of growth of population has been in the declining trend it has not influenced in anyway to boost the economy of the state. Orissa still

Table 4

Per capita Income and Percentage of People below Poverty Line among the States of India: 1999-2000

States	*Per cent of People*	*Per capita Income Current Prices Rs.*
Andhra Pradesh	15.8	14,715
Assam	36.1	9,720
Bihar	42.6	5,540
Gujarat	14.1	*16,251
Haryana	8.7	21,114
Karnataka	20.0	16,343
Kerala	12.7	*11,936
Madhya Pradesh	37.4	11,244
Maharastra	25.0	23,396
Orissa	47.2	8,733
Punjab	6.2	23,040
Rajasthan	15.3	12,533
Tamil Nadu	36.6	19,141
Uttar Pradesh	34.4	9,765
West Bengal	27.0	15,569

Source: Economic Survey, Orissa, 2001-02, Government of Orissa, Bhubaneswar.

Note: Figures for 1997-98.

remains as one of the most backward state of India even after half a century of planned development. Factors other than population growth seem to be the main cause of slow economic development which requires intensive study.

References

Census of India 2001, Orissa, Series 22, Paper 2 of 2001, Census Operations, Orissa, Bhubaneswar.

Economic Survey, India, 1999-2000, Govt. of India, New Delhi.

Economic Survey, Orissa, Economic Survey, 2001-2002, Government of Orissa, Bhubaneswar.

Statistical Outline of India, 2000-2001, Tata Services Ltd., Mumbai, 2001.

2

Population Explosion: A Comparative Analysis

— *D.Tata Rao & R.N. Misra*

Introduction

Population explosion is a burning problem of India. The nature has given us the air, the land and all other resources with limited means. Unless a check has been made on the growth of population, no doubt India will over take China, and we will face starting from food problem to all other problems as survival like a man is a big question in the year 2025.

An attempt has been made to analyse the population data of the world, China and India. Further in India the population of two neighbouring states namely Andhra Pradesh and Orissa is also taken for study. Basing on conclusions drawn from such analysis suitable suggestions are put forth for overcoming the problem of population explosion.

Population of World Vs. India

The expectation of population growth of world and India in comparison from the year 2001 to 2050 is exhibited in the Table 1.

It is expected in 2001, the world population is 610 crores and its 102.7 crores for India, but the share of India's population in the world is 16.7 per cent. But it is expected by the year 2050 the world population will be 930 crores and India's will be 162 crores. The share of India will be 17.4 per cent.

Table 1

World Bank U.N.P.O. Expectation of Population

(Population in Crores)

Years	*Population of World*	*India*	*% of Indian population*
2001	610	102.7	16.7
2015	710	126	17.7
2025	789	141	17.8
2050	930	162	17.4

Source: Vaarta a daily telugu news paper, spl. Booklet of 8-5-2001

Growth of Population in India

The growth of population of India has become more than four fold during 2001 when compared with 1901. The detailed data is exhibited in the Fig. 1.

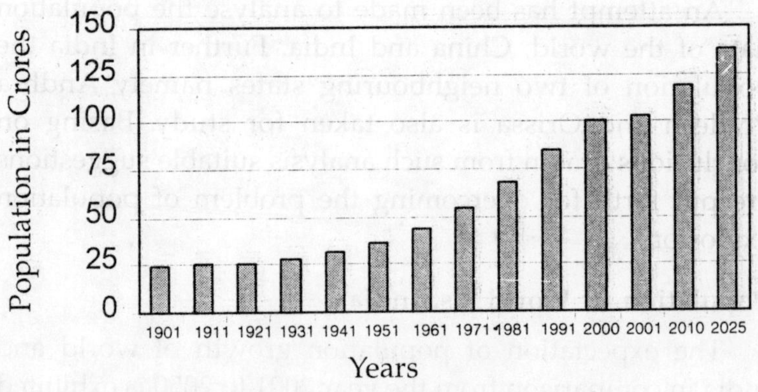

Fig. 1. India Coping with Population Explosion

The above figure 1 reveals that the population of India is in increasing trend from the year 1901 to 2001. But in the year 1921 the growth of population is slightly decreased, from the year 1911 to 1921(i.e. 0.08 crores). There was a high growth of population from the year 1961 to 2001 i.e. from 43.92 crores to 102.7 crores. India's population crossed the one billion mark on May, 11, 2000, which is 16 per cent of the world's population living on 2.4 per cent of the globe's land area. Global population increases three fold in the last century, whereas it grow five times in India. If the current trends continue, India will over take China in 2045 to become the most populated country in the world. India's population will become 1.107 million in 2010.

Comparison the Population of China, with India

We have taken a comparison of India's population with China, and taking various factors into account. Those are shown or executed in the Table-2.

The Table 2 reveals that China has stood in the First place in the world in respect of population. Whereas India occupies the 2nd place. The PGR of China is 10.6, whereas it is almost double in India (21.34). The density of population of China is much lower figure of 130 whereas in India it is 324 representing nearly 2.5 times of China. The literacy rate of China is better than that of India. The rate fertility of India is 3.3 which is almost double of China. The life expectancy is higher in China than India. The birth rate and death rate in China are less than that of India. Even the gap between the two is 8.77 for China and whereas 17.4 for India that is almost double.

Table 2

Population of China and India will other Factors

Particulars	*China*	*India*
Total population	12,7,28,52,184	102,70,15,247
Population Growth Rate	10.6	21.34
Density of population (sq.km)	130	324
Total literacy	82.9	65.38
Fertility Rate	1.76	3.3
Life expectancy	69.8	62.6
Birth Rate (per 1,000)	15.23	26.4
Death Rate (per 1,000)	6.46	9.0
Infant death rate (per, 1000)	38.0	60.8
Hospital births (per birth)	384.0	1,357.0
Doctor (per individual)	628	2,173
Land in sq. km.	37,05,460	12,69,300
Per capita (GDP & Dollar)	3,460	1,600
Below poverty line	3,81,00,000	26,20,00,000

Source: VAARTA Daily news paper, dt. 8.4.2001, Sunday supplementary.

The infant mortality rate is less in China, where as it is one and half times more in India. There are 62.8 average population per a doctor in China, where as it is more than three fold in India. Similarly 384 persons on average age a birth in hospitals in China but in India 1,357 people are to use a birth. China has more land i.e. three times of India's land, but in comparison to population China has only 16 per cent more. It means India having more population with less land. Hence the G.D.P of India less than that of China (i.e. 50% less). In view of poverty line India has a eight folds than that of China. Hence in any way China has a good economic position and also in sound developing position in comparison to India.

Population of India, Andhra Pradesh and Orissa

The population growth rate of Andhra Pradesh along with India from the year 1951 to 2001 is explained in the Figure 2.

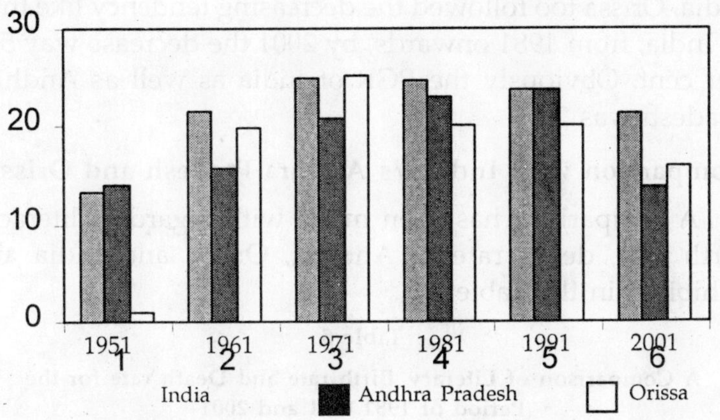

Source: Vorta Daily on 8.4.2001, Sunday, special Booklet and census report of Orissa, 2001.

Fig. 2. Population Growth of India, Andhra Pradesh and Orissa

As per the Fig 2 it reveals that as per 1951 census report the PGR of Andhra Pradesh was 14, where as it was 13.3 in India. Thus the PGR is slightly increased in Andhra Pradesh, when compared with that of India. By 1961 the PGR of India is increased to 21.5. While it was 15.7 in respect of Andhra Pradesh. Orissa ran between these two figures 19.9. Interestingly the increase in the PGR of India was 8.2, where as for Andhra it was just 1.7 from 1951 to 1961 from 1961 to 1971, the PGR of India registered 24.8 (an increase of 3.37), where as for Andhra Pradesh it was 20.9 (an increase of 5.2) for Orissa the increasing PGR is also 5.2 as the PGR registered 25.1. The PGR of Orissa is more than that of by 0.3 per cent increased in comparison to India.

From 1981 onwards the PGR of India showed a gradual decreasing tendency till 2001. But for Andhra Pradesh it showed an increasing tendency upto 1991 with 23.8 per cent. But the census of 2001 year revealed a short decline of 10 per cent which is highest among all the states of India. Orissa too followed the decreasing tendency like that of India, from 1981 onwards, by 2001 the decrease way 5.4 per cent. Obviously the PGR of India as well as Andhra Pradesh was 23.8.

Comparison with India Vs Andhra Pradesh and Orissa

A comparison has been made with regard to literacy, birth rate, death rate of Andhra, Orissa and India are exhibited in the Table 3.

Table 3

A Comparison of Literacy, Birth rate and Death rate for the Period of 1981,1991 and 2001

Particulars	*Orissa*			*Andhra Pradesh*			*Whole India*		
	1981	*1991*	*2001*	*1981*	*1991*	*2001*	*1981*	*1991*	*2001*
1. Poverty				43.6	31.7		48.3	29.9	
2. Literacy	34.12	49.1	63.61	35.7	44.1		43.7	52.1	65.38
3. Gross Birth rate			97.0	31.6	25.8		33.8	29.9	26.4
4. Infant's death rate (per 1,000)				86.0	73.0		110.0	80.0	60.8
5. Women's Ratio (per 1,000)	981	971	972	975	972		935	927	
6. Women Literacy (per 1,000)		449.7	54.1	24.2	32.7		29.8	39.3	

Source: 1. JANMA BHOOM, Margadarsaka Nirvahaha Sutralu, A booklet of Govt. of Andhra Pradesh, dt. 15-12-1997

2. Statistical out line of Orissa, 1995, Directorate of Economics and Statistics, Orissa, Bhubaneswar.

3. Provisional population totals, census 2001, series 22, Orissa, Directorate of census operations, Orissa.

The Table 3 reveals that the birth rate of Andhra is shown a declining trend in comparison to Indian census figure of 1981, 1991 and 2001. The infant death rate of the Andhra Pradesh is far behind than India. During the year 1981 the infant death rate was 86 per 1,000 but in India it was 110, similarly 73 in 1991, but in India it was 80. But in birth rate also it was 25.8 in the year 1991 in Andhra Pradesh. But it was 29.9 in India. In literacy in the census figure 1981, 1991 the Andhra Pradesh is below in comparison to India. But in all other cases India is higher than Andhra Pradesh. Though the literacy and poverty is low in Andhra Pradesh in comparison to India, but the birth rate and infant death rate is less in Andhra Pradesh.

So the poverty and illiteracy will not be taken into consideration for growth of population.

Conclusion

The population of India was 23.84 crores, during the year 1901. But the same has become four folds during 2000. If it will continue, it may increase 138 crores in 2025. So positive steps have to be taken to control this population growth. When the growth rate of India was 13.3 during the year 1951, it was 14.0 in Andhra Pradesh. But after the census period of 1961, 1971, 1983 the growth of population in Andhra Pradesh shows a decreasing trend. But in the 1991 census the growth rate of population in India was same with the growth rate of population of Andhra Pradesh. But in 2001 the growth rate of Andhra Pradesh comes to 13.8. In the year 2001, the growth rate of India is 21.3.

Though the people of Andhra Pradesh are higher in poverty in comparison to India and also literacy is higher than the Indian figure (table 2), but the growth of birth rate is less in comparison to India, in Andhra Pradesh.

Though the population of China is higher then India, but the density of population of China is much lesser than India. But in case of below poverty line the ratio between China and India is 381:2620.

3
Role of Fertility Control in Population and Environment

—Nakshatramala Panigrahi

When India had stable population of about 25 crores at the beginning of twentieth century, it had at its advancement and thought to be a heaven in every respect. Only once, its population more than to 54.82 crores by 1971 when the people had to die as a result of environmental pollution and lack of food and water. But as of now, its population has crossed 100 crore of world population though the land area is 1/6th of the world. It has been calculated that the carrying capacity of earth is 2 billion, if every individual consumes and enjoys what every U.S. people enjoy, but today world population has reached 6 billion. So there is deficit of everything and inequality from country to country and person to person increased.

The population explosion has created many problem, first and foremost being the rapid environmental pollution.

Air Pollution

Pollution of air leads to 6 per cent of all death, whereas water pollution alone kills about 12 million people of the world. It deserves mention here that the fresh water of the world is limited in quantity. The availability of fresh water for individual had reduced from 9 litres to 7 litres from 1989 to 1998. If population growth is not put under control by 2025, the per capita availability of water will come below 1000 cc in about 50 countries. With growth of population, food production is increased but not in the same rate. In the process of increasing food production, if there is use of different organic materials and pesticides which have heavy metals and chemicals, it endangers the reproductive health. Many forests are cut for agricultural land and habitation. Forests are lifeline of the Earth, as they lead to environmental syndrome which constitute global warming, climate change, which leads to increased infectious diseases, inadequate unhygienic food, landslides, floods, ozone depletion. This pases the way for ultraviolet radiation thereby resulting in increased cases of skin cancer and ocular defect.

Acid emission and acid rain are responsible for:

— Respiratory infection
— Decrease in aquatic life
— Decrease in food products
— Death of pollinators
— Leading to decrease in medicinal plant growth and, on the other hand, increased growth of dangerous algae.
— Food shortage
— Limited cultivable land, shrinking of family farm, soil erosion and degradation.
— People have to suffer from malnutrition and various diseases. About 204 million people in India are malnourished.

— Decline in ocean and coral reef, which leads to fall in aquatic life and medicinal plants.

All these may lead to loss of biological resources—in that case, people are likely to suffer from polluted food and drink. The answer to solve this problem is fertility control. The demographers have said when growth rate of population is more than 2 per cent the human development index is 0.4, but when the growth rate is less than 0.5 the human development index is one.

Methods of Fertility Control

Following are different methods of fertility control.

Permanent	*Failure rate*	*Temporary*	*Failure Rate*
Vasectomy	0.1 to 1 per cent	Natural family planning method	20 to 40 per cent
Conventional method and no scalpel vasectomy		Barrier Method	15 to 20 per cent
Tubectomy	02 to 2 per cent	Non-hormonal contraceptive cent-chrome	0.5 to 2 per cent
Minilap		Gossipal Male pill	4 to 5 per cent
Laproscopic	1 to 2 per cent	O. C. Pill	
Hysteroscopic blocking Tubal ostium	4 per cent	Combine, Triphagic, Monophagic, Sequential once a month-ORU 486	01 to 0.3 per cent
Injectable		I.U.C.D	1 to 3 per cent
Norstate - 2 months			
DMPA - 3 months			
Norplants	05 to 2 per cent		
Breast feeding			

Barrier method prevents STD, like HIV.

— Oral contraceptive increases haemoglobin concentration of women.

— Prevents cases like ovarian and uterine cancer.

Unfortunately the Vedic methods of natural fertility control by different postures of sex act, culture, custom which are as old as 4000 B.C had been forgotten by our people.

The natural methods are:

— Residential school upto completion of education.

— Swayambara marriage prevented early marriage and consequently, teen age pregnancy as well.

— Similarly, Banaprastha after attaining fifty years, prevented old age pregnancy.

Delaying Motherhood

— Marriage at 20 (Female) 25 (Male) prevents teen age pregnancy which has 2 times more maternal, prenatal and infant mortality. Old age pregnancy resulted increased birth defects, five fold risk of maternal death. Old age pregnancy can be prevented by vasectomy on tubectomy. Females exceeding 22 years of age and less than 45, males more than 30, less than 50 years are eligible for permanent methods. If the mother is having more than four children, then maternal prenatal and infant mortality is 1.5 to 3 fold.

Spacing

Spacing is essential if there is a gap between two children. In that case the prenatal maternal mortality is two fold. Spacing is obtained by different methods of temporary contraception. M.T.P. is legalised since 1972 in India to terminate unintended pregnancy. There are about 15 million abortions being carried out, of which 4-5 million abortions are done outside the proper medical service, which leads to 100-600 maternal death for 10,000 abortions-13 per cent of maternal death.

Breast Feeding

If breast feeding is done exclusively for two years, it may prevent 50 per cent of unintended pregnancy, more so it prevents breast cancer. Though the technology and methods have been greatly advanced, the birth rate has not fallen significantly nor the maternal prenatal and infant mortality. The only advantage it has shown a control on female foeticide which is decreasing the female ration day by day. Again it has increased more and more wedlock pregnancy. The next point to be noted in this regard, is all these methods are only practicable in cities and among educated people. It has not reached the people who actually require, thus it resulted fall in intelligent mass. Recent observation reveals that mostly the Hindus and affluent people are practising contraception but not the Muslims or Christians. So the Hindu population is falling day by day. Now we have to consider how to achieve the goal to check the menace of population explosion.

Measures to Check Population Explosion

I. Advocacy of false rumours against the family planning is well advocated than the benefit. For that, the family planning workers should enjoy good rapport with media, journalists to focus on the benefit of fertility control.

II. Sex education should be made compulsory in higher secondary schools, so that we can prevent teen age pregnancy and wedlock pregnancy.

III. Similar education of people will clarify everything, they will come forward to choose their own contraceptive.

IV. Quality control and proper service specially to out reach areas can only solve the problem.

V. Inadequate funding as well as inadequate contraceptive supply sometimes create the gap. For example, 24 million condoms are required for a year, whereas only 3 million condoms are procured which hardly serves the purpose.

VI. Family planning service should reach every couple until they are conscious enough to choose themselves.

VII. Proper counselling and screening allowing the people to have their own contraception choice. The family planning service provider should have proper training to screen and counsel the couple so as to remove existing myths from the society.

VIII. Quality control of service and contraceptive products can prevent much of side effects and thereby can popularise the methods.

IX Postcontraceptive followup is considered to be the most important for effective implementation.

X. Lack of male involvement and women's status in family, considerably hampers the effectiveness of programme. Out of 24-26 per cent permanent contraception, Vasectomy is only 1-2 per cent. Similarly the female usually has no voice in the home to make a choice regarding family planning method except getting pregnant.

XI. Non-involvement of private medical facilities in programme is one of the points for lessening the success rate. What we feel, is that the counselling should be a cafeteria approach. The N.G.Os and professional bodies should approach the

Government for honest utilise fund, to increase timely release of funds, which helps in smooth conduct of the work. Evaluation and punishment to negligence should be key for making the programme successful.

Jawaharlal Nehru once said, "To awaken people, it is the women who must be awakened. Once she is on move the family moves, the village moves, the nation moves." No women can call herself free until she can make a choice consciously whether she will be or will not be a mother.

4
Problems of Population Growth in India and Orissa

— R.L.Panigrahy

The proportion of elderly population in India is much higher than in South Asia as a whole. India has crossed the population of 1 billion in 2001. It was 181 crores in 1999. It is found that the average growth of 2.1% till 1991 rather diminished to 1.9% in 2001 census. The Indian Planning Commission is targeting to reduce it to 1.6% during current decade. The Indian population as on 2001 was 1,027,738 which consisted of 531,277,078 male and 4,95,738,69 female. The population growth at a rapid rate starts after independence, that is found from 1951 onwards. Before that there was a very slow growth rate of population which visualises from the .Table 1.

So, from the Table 1 it is clear that the galloping population growth rate starts from 1931 and higher growth rate starts after 1951. But within 1991 and 2001 it is slightly diminished. Because, in this period the rapid growth of population feel to the Indian people as a retarding factor not only to the.nation but also to them individually.

Due to high fertility (birth) rate and low mortality (death) rate of population creates rapid growth of

Table 1

Increase / Decrease of Population Growth in India

Year of Census	*Population in Lakhs*	*Decadal decrease/ increase in Lakhs*	*Percentage increase/ decrease in decade*	*growth rate*	*over 1991 census*
1901	2384				
1911	2521	137	5.75	0.56	575.00
1921	2513	8	-0.30	-0 .03	5.43
1931	2790	277	11.00	1.06	17.02
1941	3187	397	14.23	1.24	33.65
1951	3611	427	13.31	1.26	51.47
1961	4392	781	21.64	1.93	84.25
1971	5482	1090	24.80	2.24	129.94
1981	6852	1370	25.00	2.28	186.64
1991	8463	1611	23.50	2.14	254.00
2001	10270	—	21.34	2.00	—

Source : Census Report of India

population. Till 1921 both fertility and mortality rate of India was high. It was the first stage of demographic transition according to the economist sax. This stage continues till 1951. Since, 1951 India is in the third stage of demographic transition due to high birth rate and low death rate as the birth/death rate table is illustrated in Table 2.

The table No. 3 depicts that the demographic assessment of India, suggests a quite steep rise in the elderly population in the coming decades as a result of declining fertility and mortality. The drastic change in the composition of population and growing elderly population have far-reaching effects on the people as well as policies and priorities of the Government. Though the aging is not so serious like advanced nations, the underlying demographic process leading to aging of population has already started in India, so the problems associated with the issue are likely

Table 2

Birth and Death rate of Population in India

Period	*Annual birth rate per 1000 population*	*Annual death rate per 1000*	*Rate of increase*
1901-10	49.2	42.6	66.0
1911-20	48.1	48.6	-0.6
1921-30	46.4	36.3	10.1
1931-40	45.2	31.2	14.0
1941-50	39.9	27.4	12.5
1951-60	41.7	22.8	18.9
1961-70	41.2	19.0	22.0
1971.80	37.2	15.0	22.2
1981-86	33.2	12.2	21.0
1986-91	30.9	10.8	20.1

Source: Census Report of India.

In comparison to the countries like China, Sri Lanka, USA, UK, Sweden, etc. India has a high growth rate of population. According to 1991 census.

Table 3

Global Figure of Population in India

Country	*Rate of growth of population*
Germany	10%
Japan	10%
USA	14%
UK	14%
Sweden	14%
India	21%

Source: Indian Economic Problems of Development & Planning, Agarwal A.N.

to surface within the first two decades of 21st Century. Successes in reducing fertility and mortality and in

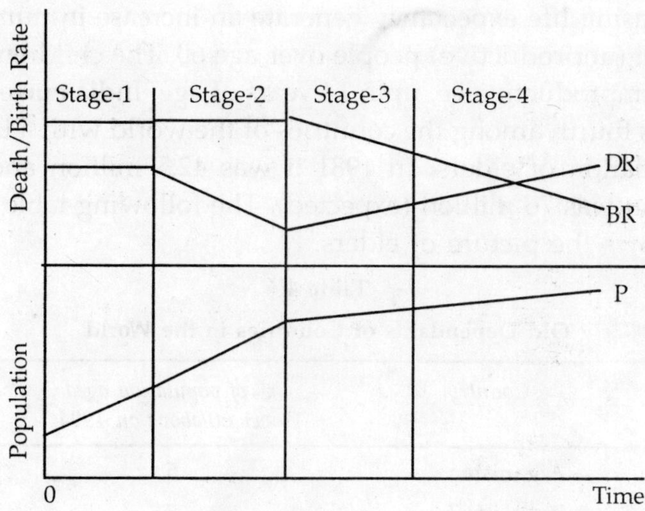

Fig. 1

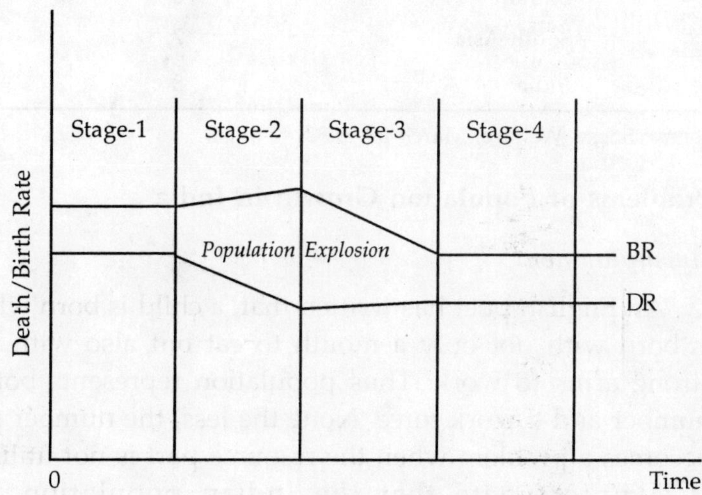

Fig. 2

Note: BR—Birth Rate
DR—Death Rate
P—Population

increasing life expectancy generate an increase in number of old (unproductive) people over age 60. The children are also unproductive i.e. upto 14 years of age. India currently ranks fourth among the countries of the world with a large population of elders. In 1981 it was 42.5 million and in 2001 it was 76 million (expected). The following table No. 4 shows the picture of elders.

Table 4

Old Dependants of Countries in the World

Country	*% of population aged over 60/above on 1994*
Afganistan	5
Bangladesh	5
Pakistan	5
Nepal	5
Bhutan	6
South Asia	7
India	8

Source: Social Welfare, March 97, p.32.

Problems of Population Growth in India

Unemployment

An English poet has written that, a child is born which is born with not only a mouth to eat but also with two strong arms to work. Thus population represents both a number and a work force. None the less, the number part becomes a problem when the resource part is not utilised. It is unfortunate that the Indian population and Development Planning is a thread of treating population as a potential resource or input needed for economic exploration to produce goods and services. But it is found as a source of unemployment and poverty. It is a liability rather than an asset. So, most of the productive age of Indian population is unproductive. The clear Indian population explosion picture is given in Table 5 and Table 6 on pages 32 and 34.

Lopsided Policy Measures

Policies of the country are largely responsible for this state of affair. The family welfare/family planning measures are treating not in proper manner for problem solving, so sometimes by some economists it is treated as villain which produces undesirable result. A deeper analysis of the issue would reveal that population is innocent and it does not stand in the way of economic progress as it is made out by demographers and Malthusians. The population as demographic entity and production economic entity are closely related with each other. Indian demography and production are negatively correlated. It not only is a problem but also adversely affected on environment and eco-system.

Poverty

The population policy planners never bothered about the number part. In India, the population is only in quantity but not in quality. All the family members share the same accommodation, food, cloth and all other amenities of life, with the number of members with the limited source of income. This process gradually shares the income and properties towards poverty. There are the drawbacks that the eligible couples belonging to the poverty-striken states are largely untouched by the population policy planners. No realistic survey has been done to list the eligible couples in any area. There is the defect of the family planning campaign is that the eligible couples among the poor are not covered as much as the non-eligible person who are

Table 5

Population, Decadal Growth and Average Exponential Growth Rate 1991 Census

Sl No.	*States/UTs*	*Population 1991 Census*	*Decadal Growth Rate 1981-91*	*1971-81*	*Average Annual Exponential Growth Rate 1981-91*	*1971-81*
1	*2*	*3*	*4*	*5*	*6*	*7*
States						
1	Andhra Pradesh	66,304,854	23.82	23.10	2.14	2.10
2	Arunachal Pradesh	858,392	35.86	35.15	3.06	3.04
3	Assam	22,294,562	23.58	23.36	2.12	2.12
4	Bihar	86,338,853	23.49	24.06	2.11	2.17
5	Goa	1,163,622	15.96	26.74	4.48	2.37
6	Gujarat	41,174,060	20.80	27.67	1.89	2.46
7	Haryana	16,317,715	26.28	28.75	2.33	2.55
8	Himachal Pradesh	5,111,079	19.39	23.71	1.77	2.15
9	J&K	7,718,700	28.92	29.69	2.58	2.58
10	Karnataka	44,817,398	20.69	26.75	1.88	2.39
11	Kerala	29,011,237	13.98	19.24	1.31	1.77
12	Madhya Pradesh	66,135,862	26.75	25.27	2.37	2.27
13	Maharashtra	78,706,719	25.36	24.54	2.26	2.21
14	Manipur	1,826,714	28.56	32.46	2.51	2.83
15	Meghalaya	1,760,626	31.80	32.04	2.76	2.80
16	Mizoram	686,217	38.98	48.55	3.29	3.99
17	Nagaland	1.215,573	56.86	50.05	4.50	4.09
18	Orissa	31,512,070	19.50	20.17	1.78	1.85
19	Punjab	20,190	20.26	23.89	1.85	2.16
20	Rajasthan	43,880,640	28.07	32.97	2.47	2.87
21	Sikkim	403,612	27.57	50.77	2.43	4.14
22	Tamil Nadu	55,638,318	14.94	17.50	1.39	1.63
23	Tripura	2,744,827	33.69	31.92	2.90	2.79

Contd.

1	2	3	4	5	6	7
24	Uttar Pradesh	138,760,417	25.16	25.49	2.24	2.29
25	West Bengal	67,982,732	24.55	23.17	2.20	2.10
Union Territories						
1	A & N Island	277,989	47.29	63.93	3.87	4.98
2	Chandigarh	640,725	41.88	75.55	3.50	5.67
3	D&N Haveli	138,542	33.63	39.78	2.90	3.38
4	Daman & Diu	101,439	28.43	26.07	2.50	2.32
5	Delhi	9,370,475	50.64	53.00	4.10	4.29
6	Lakshdweep	51,681	28.40	26.53	2.50	2.37
7	Pondicherry	789,416	30.60	28.15	2.67	2.50
All India		843,930.861	23.50	24.66	2.11	2.22

= *Projected figures as Census has not yet been conducted in Jammu & Kashmir*

= *Provisional Population Totals*

Source: Annual Report (91-92) of the Ministry of Health & Family Welfare GOI, ND, 1993

often old, unmarried, beggars, vagabonds, etc. They are brought from the vicinity of railway station, bus stands, hotels, restaurants, etc. Further, doctors in the family welfare clinics do not verify when women come for tubectomy whether their men have had vasectomy.

Indian Population—Quantity vs. Quality

The population planning strategy designed and put through hitherto has produced a ground reality where population of high quality is getting reduced gradually and corresponding population of poor quality is being increased. The awareness should be created by the campaigns as also on their violations, the intelligentsia and well-to-do sections have adopted the small family norms while the illiterate and poor sections continue to proliferate

Table 6

Selected Indicators Influencing the Birth Rate of Major States in India

Sl. No.	*Major States*	*Population in Millions*	*Birth rate 1991*	*Female Litracy Rate cenus*	*Age at Marriage 1981 Female Year Book 1989-90*	*Institutional Delivery (1989)*	*Infant Mortality Rate 1991 Source SRS*	*Mean age Accept-ance IUD in 1988-89 Year Book 1989-90*	*Mean age Accept-ance of Tubectomy in 1988-89*	*Couple Protection Rate 1990%*	*Total Fertility Rate 1989*	*1989-90 per capita Income Price (in Rs.)*
	1	*2*	*3*	*4*	*5*	*6*	*7*	*8*	*9*	*10*	*11*	*12*
1.	Kerala	29.0	18.1	86.9 (1)	21.85(1)	85.7 (1)	17 (1)	25.9 (2)	28.7 (2)	55.4 (5)	2.0(1)	3389 (8)
2.	Tamil Nadu	55.6	20.7	52.3 (2)	20.22 (3)	48.7 (2)	57 (3)	26.5 (5)	28.7 (3)	57.3 (2)	2.5 (2)	3894 (7)
3.	Andhra Pradesh	66.5	26.0	33.7(11)	17.25 (11)	32.8 (4)	73 (8)	25.5 (1)	28.4 (1)	45.3(8)	3.1 (3)	3211(9)
4.	Maharashtra	78.7	26.2	50.5 (3)	18.76(8)	33.3 (3)	60 (4)	27.8(11)	29.5 (6)	55.3 (6)	3.4 (5)	6184 (2)
5.	West Bengal	68.0	26.7	47.2 (6)	19.26 (5)	29.6 (6)	70 (7)	27.1 (9)	29.1 (5)	34.1(11)	3.3 (4)	3963(6)
6.	Karnataka	44.8	26.8	44.3 (7)	19.20 (6)	30.3 (5)	77 (10)	26.4 (3)	28.6 (4)	48.2 (7)	3.3(4)	4075 (5)
7.	Gujarat	41.2	27.5	48.5 (5)	19.51 (4)	21.6(7)	69 (6)	27.5 (10)	29.9 (8)	57.0 (3)	3.6 (6)	5404 (3)
8.	Punjab	20.2	28.6	49.7 (4)	21.04 (2)	6.8 (13)	53 (2)	26.1 (4)	31.7 (13)	73.6 (1)	3.3 (4)	7081 (1)

Contd.

1	2	3	4	5	6	7	8	9	10	11	12
9. Orissa	31.5	28.8	34.4 (10)	19.04 (7)	8.4 (12)	126 (15)	26.7 (7)	30.5 (9)	40.2 (9)	3.6 (6)	2438 (14
10. Bihar	86.3	30.5	23.1 (14)	16.52 (12)	11.3 (11)	69 (9)	27.0 (8)	31.4 (12)	24.7 (15)	5.1 (9)	2122 (15)
11. Assam	22.3	30.9	43.7(8)	NA	17.3 (9)	81 (12)	28.2 (13)	32.7(15)	27.6 (14)	3.4 (5)	2756* (12)
12. Haryana	16.3	33.1	40.9 (9)	17.87 (9)	17.9 (8)	68 (5)	29.0 (14)	31.4(11)	55.9 (4)	4.4 (7)	5274* (4)
13. Rajasthan	43.9	34.3	20.8(15)	16.09 (14)	4.2 (14)	77(11)	28.0(12)	30.7 (10)	29.5(13)	4.7 (8)	2923* (11)
14. Uttar Pradesh	139.0	35.1	26.0(13)	17.77 (10)	3.9 (15)	93 (12)	33.9(15)	32.5(14)	33.7 (12)	5.2 (10)	3072 (10)
15. Madhya Pradesh	66.1	35.8	28.8 (12)	16.52(13)	1 1.5 (10)	122(14)	26.6(6)	29.8 (7)	38.8 (10)	4.7 (8)	2739* (13)
16. All India		29.3	39.4	18.32		80.0	29.0	29.9	43.5		

**** Major States– States with a population exceeding ten million.*

States are arranged in ascending order or CBR figures

Brackets indicate comparative performance lelel.

Source: I) *Govt. of India Letter no. 11015/2/E&I dated 25.12.95*

ii) *Year Book 1989-90 Ministry of Health and Family Welfare, Government of India.*

children. The rapid growth of population is ominous signals that we shall have a social order in future which will be quantitatively more and qualitatively less. This dichotomy if allowed to grow unchecked, would land the country with poorer human resource endowment. It is high time that this trend is reversed.

Lack of Nutrition and High Fertility

It is another dimension to the population problem. It is empirically observed that woman of poor nutritional status are found to procreate more number of children. It only supports the view that, poverty is the breeding ground for population explosion. Nutritional scientists found front their research that a high degree of correlation between high nutrition and fertility rate. It emphasis that the poor families with low nutritional health conditions have big families. Hence, the increase in nutrition reduces fertility rate.

Indian Population and Socio-Economic Development

The rapid growth of population reduces the economic development of the nation as a whole. A World Bank report says that India covers Fifty Five per cent of its population below poverty line. It is found that the economic growth taking place has been cancelled by population growth. If one will go to a village, basti or urban slum including pavements the clear picture will be poverty with the faces of emaciated men and woman with unclad and unfed children in small cottages or polythene tents where the beasts will not enter, because the beasts are better housed and better fed. And how else they live and fed better without getting twice meal per day.

Negligence to Agriculture Sector

Industrialisation is required to the country for its infrastructural development in the world scenario and internal balance. Though India is an agricultural country, more than Seventy Five per cent population depend for feeding on it, how it can be neglected and run for industrialisation following western culture and thought. Though the western and advanced countries are with poor demographic transition, they depend on machine.

Our agricultural development is only with minor irrigation projects, small dams, canals, tanks under PWD management in addition to the river water and their maintenance with a long gap which does not fulfil the need of the agriculture. The industrialisation only sounds more in India. The agro-industries should be developed, so that the agricultural products will be inputted. But the agro-industries which have existence are sick and collapsed.

In India Seventy Five per cent of the agricultural land are dry which depend on rain to sow the seeds and not to think about the plough and production. So, they are unproductive.

In India, though more than Sixty per cent land ceiling legislation were enacted by states, very few are areable land. Hence agricultural development maximising employment and income has not taken place.

Economic Growth and Development

Indian economic planning practised hitherto resulting in certain growth but not in development. Growth also took place in a limited sector and that too in a limited scale affecting only the top Fifteen or Twenty per cent of Indian economy. Even this growth according to World Bank report (1988) has substantially slowed in the developing countries in India. The investments have fallen to levels in important sectors of their economy. The debts are growing. The severity surpasses that of the great depression. The basic problem of poverty and growth in the developing world can be stated simply. The growth is not suitably reached the poor and the poor are not significantly contributing to growth or development. A study of Dr. C. T. Kurien has noted that Indian Plans have produced both prosperity and poverty. Prosperity for the rich who are resourceful and poverty for the poor who are resourceless with the result that the rich have become richer and the poor become poorer. This implies that development for all have been eluded.

Indian planners have adopted the capital-intensive techniques using more of scarce capital and less of abundant labour as was in vague in western countries. It was forgotten by our chair borne economists that the western countries have followed what was dictated by their resource endowment. Our country has followed what they have followed and not as dictated by our resource endowment. The direct outcome of this is mass scale unemployment of the labour resource and large scale borrowing of capital externally and internally.

Literacy and Development

Literacy rates and per capita income levels are positively associated. All developed countries have Hundred per cent literacy. But in India, it is 65.38%. (566,714,995) with 75.85% (339,969,048) male and 54.16% (226,745,947) female population are literate. A wholly literate population will be able to participate in worth while productive factors, can be a skilled labour and can maximise productivity. Only the whole literate population can understand and be conscious on the development, sphere and problems of the country and a look for its betterment where there is poverty ridden in a country, how there are the chance of 100% literacy and expectations for development.

Unemployment

The net addition to the labour force during the period 1992-97 is estimated to be 35 million and another 36 million will be expected to an addition during 1997-2002. Thus additional employment opportunities of the order of 53 million will have to be created during 1992-1997 if the goal of near full employment is to be reached in 1997.

As the growth of population is very fast, the number of labour force entered in population as labour force seek employment. In developing countries, the job is very less than the job seekers. So, not only unemployment but also the underemployment, disguised unemployment and the engagements without remuneration (which can not be called as employment as the definition of employment) are found in India. So, what a miserable condition of the productive group of Indian population are lying neglected. It is the wastage of Indians human resources. Due to unemployment, the social problems also occur. The unemployed youth many times commits notorious works like mischief in streets, public places, pick pocketing, comment to the young girls, rape, theft, murder, love harassment effects, smuggling, prostitution, drink, etc. The unemployment multiplies lowering the growth rate of the economy of the country. Due to unemployment the per capita income of the country declines.

From 1960s to 1980s, the collapses of entrepreneurs created unemployment in India due to centralisation of industries and entrepreneurs. According to the survey of Ministry of Labour & Employment, in 1951 unemployment was 2.44 lakhs, in 1966, 9.2 lakhs, in 1972, 32.8 lakhs, in 1980, 34.8 lakhs, in 1985, 47 lakhs and so on. The unemployment also creates due to non-irrigation facilities to the agricultural lands. Total 31.3% of land holdings are irrigated out of which Twenty Five per cent are not for two crops. So, around Seventy Five per cent of land holdings are lying vacant for 4 to 6 months. It is also a cause of unemployment in rural sector.

Problems on Capital Formation

According to Dale & Hoove, "the rapid growth of population tend to diminish the amount of capital available for investment and production diminishes". According to Prof. Leibenstein, "in densely populated economies, population growth is an obstacle to development because it dilutes the amount of capital with the representative worker may operate." In India Forty to Fifty per cent of its population are in unproductive group and unemployment arises from the productive age group of 15 to 50 years. So, Prof. Meier has noticed that, "the high dependency requires the economy to divert considerable part of the resources that might, otherwise go into capital formation to the maintenance of high percentage of dependents who may never become producers". Thus, the rapid growth of population leads to diversion of capital investment from directly activities to social overhead capital. The rapid population growth tends to depress savings per capita and growth of physical capital per worker. Pepelasis and Mears who have stated that "Population increase can frequently be associated with reduction in per capita output,, the per capita surpluses potentially available for investment may actually decline". According to Prof. Keynes, saving is an investment in underdeveloped countries which ultimately will be investment. The rapid growth of population reduces saving, which reduces investment and productivity, income, economic growth in a flow. It reduces the standard of living destination to poverty. In this context, J. J. Spengler has observed, "to attain 3.2 per cent increase in per capita income, 13.8 per cent of national income must be invested in population increase by One per cent and for Two per cent increase in population, 19.5 per cent of national income must be invested. And for the same heavy source of foreign assistance is required". Thus heavy population growth retards the rate of growth of less developed countries.

Population Pressure in Orissa—at a Glance

Gandhiji exclaimed in anguish in his visit to Orissa first time in 1920, "Orissa is a epitome of India's poverty". Now we are ratting on the lowest step of poverty's ladder and have not raised ourselves beyond it. Still Orissa is poorest state in India and India is poorest in the globe. A poet expressed, poverty alone can destroy all virtues.

Table 7

Orissa at a Glance as on 2001 Census

Districts	:	30
Area	:	155,707 Sq. K.M.
Population	:	36,706,920
Male	:	18,612,340
Female	:	18,094,580
Decadal increase	:	5,047,184 (15.94%)
Density Population	:	236 per Sq. K.M.
Female/Male ratio	:	972/1000
Literacy	:	20,053,785 (63.61% in total)
Male	:	12,118,256 (75.95% of male)
Female	:	7,935,529 (50.97% of female)

Source: Utkal Prasang, May, 2002, p. 52.

In Orissa both agricultural and non-agricultural sectors provide a great reservoir of employment to rural people. Inspite of agricultural uplift and self-sufficiency in national food production, Orissa lagged behind the states viz. Punjab, Haryana, UP and so also in employment generation. A mere 30.7 per cent of the total cultivable land are irrigated by 1991. This does not facilitate multicroping the generate employment throughout the year. Poor land reforms, low technology, law irrigation are mostly responsible for unemployment in Orissa. Taking these into consideration rural people depend on the nearest urban areas on non-agricultural sectors. The non-agricultural sector as an alternative source of employment absorbs 29 per cent of rural population in Orissa. The sector includes village handicrafts and transport. There is less chances of employment in industries directly or indirectly. The industries in Orissa are sick or closed. The agro-industries are only lying their area which was in operation as a monument and some are in sick position. In this consequence, how the agricultural products can have demand in the market and employment can be generated? Besides a major portion of rural population in Orissa are daily wage earners who are unskilled, landless, illiterate/less educated, their family members are also in the same track, so that they can feed themselves twice in a day. Their necessity and ignorance force them to work at a low price and their children are available as a cheap and non-wage earning labourers. In this case, they will try to move to urban area where they have to live in pavements, foot tracks, central bus stand and railway platforms as slum in a miserable condition anyway to live. From the currant scenario the rural unemployment reservoir is so acute that the model of Prof. Lewis is impractical in case of Orissa. In spite of liberalisation and privatisation the urban industrial sectors are unable to absorb the total rural labour surplus in Orissa. As on the Economic Survey of Government of Orissa, the total unemployment reservoir of Orissa was

7.13 Lakhs in 1994-95 and it was found around 2.5 lakh unemployment creates per annum.

Unemployment and abysmal living condition of the poor in rural areas are the two main problems to be attacked. So, rapid action plans in curbing these maladies are warranted the spread of irrigation facilities through large medium and minor irrigation schemes and sustained effort for multi-cropping. Several rural development and employment generations programmes-schemes to be launched/implemented in the rural sector aiming for employment generation. The effort should be taken to divert the corrupt village leaders. The urban industrial sectors of Orissa (around 40%) are inadequate to absorb all the surplus rural unemployment. The awareness, education, consciousness and competition vigour of the villages to be improved with several orientation programmes to uplift the rural unemployed and the people in poverty.

Conclusion

In India in the name of economic development, economic growth occurs. The growing population reduces the economic development to economic growth. In last 54 years of independence, definitely rapid growth found out, but the rapid growth population diminishes it.

Despite almost every economist and demographic producing realms of reports on the mal-effects of a high fertility rate and even though politicians in power are also fully conscious of the consequences of the population explosion, this subject gets much attention from very important persons or media as a measure to make the people conscious. On the other hand, subjects like inflation, environmental degradation, bio-diversity, religious intolerance, devaluation, etc. are the high level debates due to rapid growth of Indian population.

So, the mass media have to continue to play their role of increasing awareness and creating the atmosphere for the acceptance of the programme. But they can not change ways of people. At best they can take the horse to water, but can not make it drink. The role has played by the people themselves, NGOs, family groups and the opinion leaders on whom the people rely for advise and help. The contraceptive and Intra Uterine Devices (IUD) as the birth control devices should be introduced to the people, mostly in urban slums and rural people where people breed like flies under sub-human conditions.

The root cause of rapid growth of population that creates problem to the economy is high fertility rate due to low nutritious food, low mortality rate, illiteracy mostly among women, women's low status, custom of preference for male child, early and child marriage, poverty and slum etc.

In this consequence, it is better for the demographic planners to attempt for reducing population by attempting to make conscious among the eligible couples of poverty, malnutritious and slum. They should have a look for agricultural development, industrial development with labour intensive techniques instead of machine intensive and try to achieve hundred per cent literacy. So, the population in India can be a boon rather a bane or a retarding factor.

References

Diptivilash U., "Understanding Perspective of Population Problem" *Social Welfare*, p. 32.

Population Growth a Boon or Bane? *The Hindu*, dated 25.12.2001.

Agarwal, A.N., *Indian Economic Problems of Development & Planning*, 2000.

Grewal, P. S., *Indian Economic Problems*, 1985.

Lekhi, R.K., *The Economic Development and Planning*, 1994.

Jayasree, *Demographic Analysis of Aging, Social Welfare*, March, 1997.

Ramasamy, Dr. A.S. "Population, Environment & Development", *Kurukshetra*, March, 1996.

Panaroma Year Book 2002, p. 72.

Misra D., Panda R.C., Nature of Rural Unemployment in Orissa: An Evaluation of Govt. Programme Performance, *Orissa Review*, Feb. 1997.

India's Census 2001, Orissa's Population at a Glance, *Utkal Prasang* (Monthly Oriya Publication of Government of Orissa. Publication) May 2001.

Patil Dr. J., "Growing Population & Employment Implications in Rural Areas", *Kurukshetra*, Oct., 1993.

Singh, Dr. K., Five Point Strategy of Stem Population, *ibid.*, p.17.

Bhatt, S.C., "Precious time last: let's get a move on", *ibid.*, p.30.

Gupta, Dr. D.P., "Needing Improved Health Care to Fight Population Explosion", *ibid.*, p. 41

Antony, T.V., Countering Population Explosion, *ibid.*, p. 45.

Kurup, Dr. R.S. "Curbing population Growth", *ibid.*, p. 59.

Panigrahy, Dr. D. D., Bekara Samasya (Unemployment Problem), *Yojana*, (Oriya) July 1994, p. 9.

Bhuyan, Dasarathi, A Study of Political Contribution & Personality of Sri Janaki Ballav Patnaik, Chief Minister of Orissa (Ph.D. thesis) 2001, p. 174.

Das, B.P., "Ama Rajya tatha desharu daridrya hataiba sambhabapara" (Possibility of eradication of poverty from our state and country), *Anupama Bharat* (Oriya daily) dated 18.6.2002.

5

Population and Enviromental Pollution

— Santosh Kumar Pradhan & R.N. Misra

Introduction

India, in terms of population, occupies second place in the world whereas 7th place in terms of land area. India has 2.4 per cent of world's land with 16 per cent of world's population. The present population of India is a far more than the combined population of U.S.A and U.S.S.R. These two countries have only 12 per cent of the world's population and 21.3 of world's land area.

The comparison is made simply to highlight the population problem of India which is responsible for twin deep rooted problems of proverty and unemployement in the country.

During the decade 1991-2001 India's population increased at an annual exponential growth rate of 2 per cent which is marginally less than 2.1 per cent growth rate in the previous decade of 1981-1991. India's population has grown steadily after 1921 and the growth rate has been higher after 1951. (Table 1) The progressive growth rate over 1901 reveals an explosive situation of India's population in this present century.

The Table 1 depicts the galloping population in the country. The growth of population is a function of high birth rate and less death rate, which became a problem. It pressures upon the economic, political, social as well as cultural fields.

Table 1

Growth of Population in India

Year	*Population in Million*	*Decadal Absolute*	*Growth present*	*Average Annual expponential growth rate%*	*Progressive growth rate over 1901%.*
1901	238.39	-	-	-	-
1911	252.09	13.70	5.75	0.56	5.75
1921	251.32	0.77	0.31	0.03	5.43
9131	278.97	27.65	11.00	1 .04	17.02
1941	318.66	39.69	14.22	1 .33	33.65
1951	361 .03	42.42 .	13.31	1 .25	51.47
1961	439.23	78. 15	21.51	1 .96	84.25
1971	548.15	108.92	24.80	2.20	129.94
1981	683.32	135.17	24.66	2.22	186.64
1991	846.30	162.98	23.50	2.11	254.00
2001	1027.01	—	21.34	2.00	—

Soures : United Nations World Populaton—1990-91, Statement.

The growing population is both a blessing and a curse. It is a blessing in thinly populated country as it helps in the exploitation and utilisation of natural resources and hence accelerate the pace of growth. It is a sin in over population country and retards the process of economic development.

India falls in the 2nd category as the population has been rising unabated and has accentuated the problems of

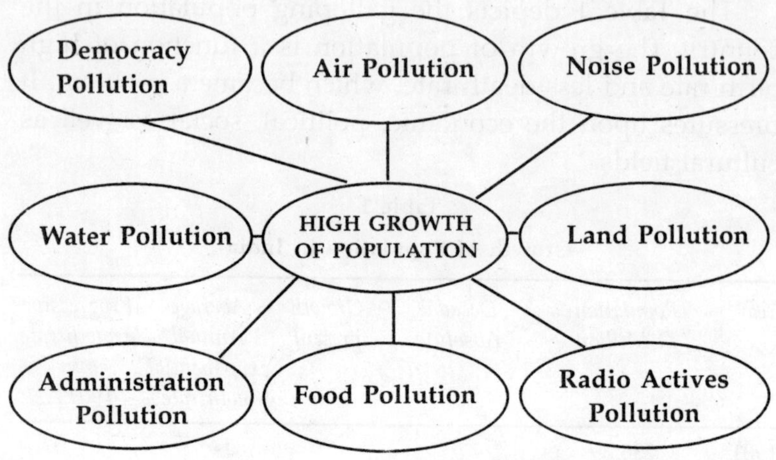

Fig 1 : Pollution due to Population Growth

every sides.

1. Fast, growing population forces the per capita income continuous to be low.
2. It has resulted in tiny and scattered holding which hinder the adoption of new farm technology.
3. It has aggravated the problems of unemployment both among the educated and uneducated.
4. It raises expenditure on social infrastructure and adversely affected on investment.
5. It blames the smooth progress of capital formation.
6. It creates large number of unproductive consumers.
7. It creates pressure on export promotion and import substitution.

Population & Pollution

Inspite of these problems we have taken a clear picture about rapidly rising population contribute to pollution of environment. Due to some activity and the part of human being or without any activities on their part, pollution is classified into natural pollution and artificial pollution.

The disorder of nature environment created nature pollution. The source of artificial pollution are by human activities, industrialisation and otherwise, from the point of view of object, pollution may be classified into different types all of these pollution held by the population explosion, which are presented on the figure No. 1.

Impact of Population Growth

Due to high growth rate of population so many solid, liquid or gaseous substance including noise, present in the atmosphere by use of vehicles, industrialisation. The problem of air pollution began to be felt in the country to be a danger.

On land terrestrial life exists terrestrial flora and fauna survive on it. The major source of land pollution is the massive amount of solid wastes disposed by human being such pollution is created by house hold refuse, coercial rubbish industrial wastes, plastic items. They are not only a nuisance value but also hazardous to health. The non-agriculture uses of land was last as precious areable land for township, park, air strips, car parks, etc. is accounted at 0.1 to 0.2 hectors per person. India has lost three per cent of forests per annum, and hence India's degraded land area are largest in the world (*source*: the earth summit in RIO in 1992)

Raising population requirement of food also increasing in this manner products of more food, use of paste, chemicals are polluted foodgrain on the other hand food became polluted during the pocessing, storage, transportation and retailing.

Property exhibited by unstable isotopes of element which decay, emiting radiation, principally alpha, beta and gama partical is known as radio activities. These radiations are biologically harmful, safest limit of radio activity to human being is 0.25 per cent per week. If it is taken in greater dose than 0.25 and if taken regularly it can cause disease like cancer, tumors, etc. Nuclear power plant and testing of atom bombs are the main sources of radio active pollution.

Noise pollution is a very interesting subject on pollution which is creating by men with the noise of vehicles, radios, T.V., tape recorders, loud speakers, etc. It is created by sound which is a mechanical energy from a vibrating surface transmitted by cyclic series of comparison and rate function of the molecules of the material through which it passes.

Water is an important constituent of life support system. In our country the main source of water is the farm presipition which roughly accounts four hundred million hector meter per year. Nearly fifty per cent of it percolate into the soil, 30 per cent of it runs in surface fun of and other 20 per cent evaporated into the atmosphere. Pure and clean water is necessary for the healthy environment. But in over populated country like India, human activities related with water pollution comprised mining, agriculture, stock breeding, fisheries, urban human activities various industries, domestic sewage.

Conclusion

The greatest achievement of Indian democracy is that despite ups and downs, it has always survived with added strength. One billion people live together as one national entity under condition of freedom. But there was a vital difference between the ancient, democracy and modern. Modern politicians are mis-utilised their democracy power after getting leadership. They cheat general people, they function their democracy power for getting profit only. Due to high growth rate of population modern politicians try to get their power by force or take over the democracy power from the general people. In the last 50 years the treamble, 13 general elections have been held which have been not only free but also fair. The Multy party system has contributed significantly to the growth of opposition which is not only the back-bone but also the bed-rock of real democracy.

Not only democracy, but also in the fields of administration senior I.A.S., I.P.S., I.E.S., I.F.S. officers are misutilised their power are getting profits. In this populated country there is a problem in every side for living peaceful. Therefore, the administration in units ready to misutilise their power and do any illegal work. So high growth rate also pollutes to the administration.

Coupled with population explostion, the hazards of environmental pollution has created a catastrophe to the man-kind. Humanity is in the grip of serious problems to maintain its existence, protection, survival and for the improvement of living standards.

References

Pradhan, N.B., *Demographic Behaviour in India.* Article presented Eigth Ganjam Economic Seminar, 1995, p. 16.

Khullar, K.K., *Indian Democracy March Employment News,* 20-26 Jan. 01.

Grewal, P.S., *Problems of Growth of Population,* p.1 4-8.

Banege, Shubhanker, Protecting environment from disaster "*Kurukshetra* Dec. 1995, p. 45.

Tewari, O.P., *Environmental Law,* pp.18, 22-28.

Tripathy S.N., Panda Sunda: *Environmental Pollution,* p. 104, 105.

6
Dimensons of Population Control in India

— D. D. Choudhury & R.C Pandit

The bulk size and the rapid growth rate of population have posed an unsurmountable problem before the nation and are now the matters of great concern for all concerned — the planners, policy makers as well as the Government. Population explosion is at the root of all economic maladies in India. The census data of 2001 reveals that the population of India exceeded 102 crores by marking an increase of 18.4 crores during the last decade which is greater than the population of Brazil the fifth largest populous state in the world. Out of this, the male population was 53.12 crores and the female population was 49.57 crores.[1] While the country is endowed with a vast panaroma of natural resources and has developed a remarkable infrastructure for Industrial progress within a span of 53 years of planned development, the per-capita income and the rate of economic growth are far from the expectation.

A study by C. Gopalan[2], reveals that nearly 15 per cent of the children born become truly healthy, physically fit, productive and intellectually capable citizens of this country. Out of the rest, majority of the children emerge into adulthood with impaired physical stamina, low productivity and poor mental abilities due to serious under-nutrition and ill-health during their childhood. Besides as is well known that the rapid growth of population inflicts problems like pressure on land, housing, unemployment, under-employment, malnutrition, burden of unproductive consumers, lowering foreign exchange reserve and finally, it also results for the deterioration of quality of human resources. Thus there is a dire need for population control.

Measures to Control

A fast growing population with a galloping speed has been experienced as deleterious as it undermines all our efforts for development. Therefore an attempt has been made here to suggest some ways and means to get over from this impasse. The measures needed to curb the rapid growth of population of our country can broadly be categorized under two heads such as Government efforts and voluntary efforts which have been discussed below.

To check the inexorable rate of growth of population, the state has to play a key role besides the existing birth control programmes launched at present. Government efforts should comprise the following.

(a) Health Measures

As is evident from the Table 1, there is a high degree positive co-ordination between mortality rate and birth rate and Birth rate and infant mortality rate. Therefore, the infant mortality rate needs to be drastically reduced. Child survival rate can be increased through the extension of medical facilities in the rural and tribal areas. The P.H.C.s, Maternity Welfare Centres, Rural Health Centres and should be opened in the rural and tribal pockets alongwith the provision of staff quarters and other facilities such as marketing, communication, electricity etc. The Doctors and other medical staffs should be insisted to stay in the Head Quarters; so that pre-natal and post natal care can be taken

Table 1

Birth Rate and Death Rate of 14 major States of India (1996)

Sl. No.	*State*	*Birth rate*	*Death rate*	*I.M.R.*	*Mean age at Marriage (Females)*
1.	Kerala	17.8	6.2	13	22.3
2.	Tamilnadu	19.2	7.9	54	20.2
3.	Andhra Pradesh	22.7	8.3	66	17.8
4.	Maharastra	23.2	7.4	48	19.1
5.	Karnataka	23	7.6	53	19.4
6.	West Bengal	22.8	7.8	55	19.5
7.	Punjab	23	7.5	52	20.3
8.	Orissa	26.8	10.7	95	19.5
9.	Gujarat	25.5	7.6	62	20.4
10.	Haryana	28.8	8.1	68	19.2
11.	Bihar	32.1	10.2	72	18.6
12.	Madhya Pradesh	32.4	11.1	97	18.8
13.	Rajasthan	32.3	9.1	86	18.4
14.	Uttar Pradesh	34.0	10.2	86	19.3
	All India	24.4	8.9	72	19.4

Source: Planning Commission, *9th Five year plan (1997-2002)*, Volume I, p. 23.

N.B.: The co-relation coefficient between birth rate and infant mortality rate is r = +0.73.

I.M.R.= Infant Mortality Rate.

intime. In the rural area a child is considered as a social security for the parents at their old age. Thus unless the child survival rate is improved it would be very tough to reduce birth rate. In Table 1 States like Kerala and Tamil Nadu have low birth rate because of low infant mortality rate which could be possible due to proper care given to the mothers and children, and improvement of literacy.

In advanced countries like Germany, U.K., U.S.A., Canada, France, besides other factors, Birth rate is low because of low mortality rate, especially low infant mortality rate and here also there is high degree positive corelation between birth rate and infant mortality rate which can be seen in Table 2.

Table 2

Crude Birth rate, Death rate for Selected Countries (1994)

Sl . No.	*Country*	*Birth rate*	*Death rate*	*I.M.R. (1995)*
1.	Germany	10	11	6
2.	U.K.	14	11	6
3.	U.S.A.	16	09	8
4.	Canada	15	07	6
5.	France	13	09	6
6.	Australia	15	08	7
7.	Japan	11	07	4
8.	China	19	08	34
9.	India	26	09	68

Source: World Development Report 1997.

Therefore, from the study of Table 1 & 2 it is understood to control Birth Rate we have to reduce the infant mortality rate.

Again infant mortality rate is also caused by nutritional deficiency which given rise to anaemia. Studies carried out in the National Institute of Nutrition, Hyderabad[3] have revealed that nearly 63 per cent of children below 3 years of age and about 45 per cent between 3 & 5 years were found to suffer from anaemia. The observations further indicate that Iron deficiency anaemia affects the brain function and thus the quality of population adversely.

Therefore, the Nutrition factor must be accorded due priority in any policy of population control.

(b) Family Planning

Family planning or family welfare programme is a revolutionary step of Government to reduce the birth rate. But compared to the family planning expenditure incurred in different plan periods it is inferred that the outcome is not commensurate to the outlay which is evident from the Table 3 & 4.

Table 3

Family Planning Expenditure in the Various Plans

Plan period	*(Rs. Crores)*	*% of the total plan outlay*
Third Plan (1961-66)	25	0.3
Annual Plans (1966-69)	70	1.1
Fourth Plan (1969-74)	278	1.8
Fifth Plan (1974-79)	492	1.2
Sixth Plan (1980-85)	1448	1.3
Seventh Plan (1985-90)	3121	1.4
Eighth Plan (1990-95)	6792	1.4

Source: Economic Survey (1996-97) and earlier issues.

Table 4

Percentage of Eligible Couple Effectively Protected by different Methods of Birth Control

Year	*Sterilisation*	*I.U.D.*	*Other methods*	*All methods*
1970-71	8.0	1.4	1.0	10.4
1976-77	20.7	1.1	1.7	23.5
1981-82	20.7	1.1	2.0	23.7
1984-85	24.9	2.9	4.4	32.1
1985-86	26.5	3.7	4.7	32.5

Source: Ruddar Dutta & K.P. M. Sundaram, *Indian Economy*, 1999, p. 64.
I.U.D.—Intra Uterine Device.

The main objective of the Family Planning which is currently known as family welfare programme is to reduce the birth rate. But it could not be successfully materialised despite of heavy expenditures incurred for the programme mainly due to lack of proper devotion and dedication of the officials, strong political will as well as the response of the people. It is more seriously viewed that effective involvement of the people is quite indispensable for the success of the Family Planning Programme. In this context Late Prime Minister Smt. Indira Gandhi has emphasized that Family Planning must become a Peoples' movement- of the people, by the people, for the people.

But those who view that Family Planning should be primary concern of the people and not of the Government is not totally valid. The success of the family planning lies with the strong political will, devotion of Government. Officials as well as active participation of the people.

For this, strong motivation is necessary which can be achieved by the field workers like village agriculture workers, village health workers, A.N.M. and other field staffs, teachers by giving them some incentives like promotion, extra increments, cheap credit facilities for house construction, reservation of seats for their children for various jobs, and Engineering and Medical Colleges apart from the incentives given to those who undergo sterilization. As mothers are more interested for sterilization, they should be motivated to undergo sterilization at the time of delivery of first or a second child. Each field worker should be assigned a quota of motivating the couples to undergo sterilization (100 cases for each field worker) after one child or at best two children, for availing incentives.[4]

(c) Literacy Improvement Measures

There is a very close relationship between literacy improvement and Birth rate. Literate couples, especially literate mothers always prefer small family than their illiterate counterparts which can be manirested in Table 5.

Table 5

No. of Children born per Woman in the Age Group of (45-49)—1991

Education level	*No. of children birth*		
	Total	*Rural*	*Urban*
Illiterate	4.4	4.4	4.3
Literate below middle.	4.3	4.4	4.1
Middle below matric	3.8	3.9	3.7
Matric but below Graduate	3.0	3.1	2.9
Graduate & above	2.3	2.6	2.2
Total	4.3	4.4	3.9

Source: Census of India State Profile 1991.

In the International literature considerable interest has been attached to Kerala which can be compared to Sri Lanka. Kerala being distinguished from other states has highest literacy rate. (i.e. 90.92 as per the census 2001), highest expectation of life. The lowest infant mortality followed by the lowest birth rate.

In India male literacy rate is 64.1 per cent (1991 Census) and Female literacy rate is 39.3 per cent and the latter is still worse in the rural areas. Therefore due emphasis should be attached for the improvement of literacy in general and for the rural women in particular. In this connection adult education programme should be implemented with much vigour and commitment, by involving the non-formal teachers and voluntary organisations. Further, health education, nutrition education, environmental education, population education should be incorporated as a part of the regular school curriculum.

(d) Other Measures

As stated earlier a child especially a male child is considered an asset as well as the security of the parents at the time of the old age in the rural areas. Therefore, social security measures in the form of employment facilities, accidential benefits, sickness benefit, adequate amount of old age pension should be provided in order to motivate them not to have more no. of children.

As poverty also accounts for high birth rate, therefore, some special anti-poverty programmes which generate employment and create non-saleable assets should be launched.

Again there should be a common civil code for all the communities living in India irrespective of caste, creed, religion with regard to Family Planning Programme. It is not just insisting one community to undergo sterilisation, living some other communities to adopt polygamy and their own socio-religious code.

Further, the census data 1991 reveals that the birth rate of Bihar, Madhya Pradesh, Uttar Pradesh and Rajsthan is greater than the all India average and the population of these four states taken together constitutes 44 per cent of the total population of our country.

So some special programmes should be designed to stunt the population growth of these states.

2. Voluntary Efforts

Mere Government effort is not enough to control the population growth in the country. Voluntary Organisations have to play a catalytic role in this regard. In the rural and the semi-urban areas motivation is the suitable weapon to check the birth rate. Mothers should be properly motivated. This should be done co-operatively by the Govt. officials and by the Voluntary Organisations which are supposed to supplement the Government efforts. More funds should be accorded to those voluntary associations which undertake the task of educating the rural women and motivate the newly married couples and create awareness about family planning in rural area. The work of the voluntary associations should be assessed at regular intervals for further grant of funds.

Besides, these Panchayats, Youth Clubs, Yubak Sanghas have also to play a key role to motivate the rural people for birth control.

Conclusion

Since there is a close relationship between fertility and educational status of women, mortality especially infant mortality and other linkage factors like increasing employment opportunities, reducing inequalities in the income and wealth, therefore birth control can not be achieved through isolated measures of family welfare. It needs a united efforts of all concerned—the Government officials, the NGOs, politicians and people.

However, reduction of Infant Mortality Rate through the opening of maternity welfare centre, P.H.C.s and improvement of medical facilities in the rural areas, improvement of literacy especially female literacy, motivation and awareness creation for birth control by the Government. Officials and voluntary Associations, extension and improvement of social security measures, providing better incentives to the field workers actively engaged in implementing family welfare programme, involvement of women in work, development of overall status of women in the society, removal of poverty by launching anti-poverty programmes, creation of a separate department for demography control will go a long way in controlling the rapid growth of population in India.

Notes

1. *Sambad*, Dtd. 27.03.2001 (Oriya Daily Newspaper).
2. *Yojana* 1983, January, 26.
3. *Ibid*.
4. Ruddar Dutt & K.P.M. Sundaram, *Indian Economy*, 1999.

7
Population Growth and Its Control

— ***Nilamadhaba Mohanty***

Population growth is both conducive to economic development and a drag on the same in various situations. In olden days, when population was very low compared to the vast masses of land in the world, growth of population was necessary. But in the recent years, population growth is largely conceived of as a drag on economic growth or even swallowing the fruits of development. An examination of their relationship therefore, requires a dynamic analysis in the various ages from time immemorial.

High birth rate supplemented with improved health and medical facilities (which makes death rate fall) pushes the economy towards the state of population explosion. India faces the same situation at present. An increasing difference between birth rate and death rate has created a scene of population explosion in India.

India has been recognised the second most overpopulated country in the demographic world. The excess going of population is due to variety of reasons.

(i) Universal Marriage

Marriage is considered to be the duty of every person in India. The Hindu society looks down upon the women who do not marry after attaining 30 years. It is estimated by Myrdal that 70 per cent of the women in the age group of 20 to 24, 94 per cent of the women in the age group of 25 to 39, 91 per cent of the women in the group of 30 to 34, and 87 per cent of the women in the age group of 35 to 39 are married in India. Thus universally of marriage in India has also contributed to the growth of population in India.

(ii) Early Marriage

Moreover due to climatic reasons, Indian girls mature between 12 and 15 years of age. Several orthodox parents like to get their daughters married immediately after they are matured. Normally, the child-bearing age of women is 15 to 45. Early marriage prolongs the child bearing age and consequently leads to a rapid growth of population.

(iii) Illiteracy, Ignorance and Superstitions

In India only 35 per cent of the people are literate. The vast majority of people are illiterate. Ignorance, traditional beliefs, customs and religious doctrines also dominate the thinking of the people to deliberately limit the size of their families. As a result population is increasing unchecked by the people in India.

(iv) Excessive Importance to Male Children

Moreover, many Indians consider that female children, are a liability while male children are an asset. They believe that only a son will look after parents during old age and that daughters will get married and leave their parents. Thus the excessive importance attached to male children is also partly responsible for the large sized families in India.

(v) Fears about Family Planning Method

Due to ignorance and illiteracy, many people in India develop apprehensions about family planning techniques. They think that the adoptation of family planning techniques, will have side effects which in the long run will be injurious to the health of the women.

On account of these reasons the population of India is growing very rapidly. Although India occupies about 2.4 of the total land area of the world but the country at present has to support nearly 16 per cent of the total population of the world. The table 1 shows the growth of population in India since 1901 to 1997.

Table 1

Growth of Population in India (1901 - 1991)

Census Year	*Rate of total Population*	*Annual growth rate*
1901	238.3	03.0
1911	252.0	0.66
1921	251.2	0.3
1931	278.9	1.06
1941	318.7	1.34
1951	360.4	1.26
1961	361.0	1.26
1971	548.2	2.2
1981	684.0	2.23
1991	843.9	2.11
1997	949.9	2.00

Source: Provisional Population 1991 and *Economic Survey of India* (1997-1998).

India is a vertiable darling of nature where there is a unity and diversity of culture, religion, language etc. Here different types of people having their different types of religion live inside India. The religion wise population has been depicted in the table 2.

The bomb of population explosion has created multidimensional problems like unemployment, poverty, disguised unemployment, problems of social infrastructure fooding and sheltering etc. Amongst which the environmental problem is by far the most important problem.

Table 2

Religion	*Population (in crs)*	*Percentage in total Population*	*Population growth during 1981-91*	*Sex ratio female per thousand male*
Hindu	68.76	82. 0	22.78	925
Muslim	10.16	12.12	32.76	930
Christian	1.96	2.34	16.89	994
Sikh	1.63	1.94	25.48	888
Buddhas	0.64	0.76	35.98	952
Jain	0.34	0.46	4.42	946
Other	0.37	0.44	13.19	-
Total Population	83.86	100.00	23.79	927

Note: Excludes Assam & Jammu & Kashmir.

In India, the problem of deforestation is very much acute. Total area under forests has been gradually declining in India due to its total mis-management. The factors which are largely responsible for large scale deforestation include growing demand for minor forest produce and fuel wood by the people, increasing demand for raw-materials for forest based industries and increasing demand for state revenue from forest. From the very beginning state

Governments were very much interested to collect a big volume of revenue by selling timber and other forest produce. Moreover, forest bureaucracy allowed illegal felling of trees with the sole intension to get illegal gratification. Besides, indiscriminate cutting of trees standing in the forest adjacent to the village by the villagers is also responsible for massive deforestation in the country. Again a good and number of landless poor are regularly cutting trees and selling firewood for earning their livelihood. In this way the pace of deforestation has been intensified since Independence.

At present experts feel to maintain ecological balance in India 20 per cent area of the plains and 60 per cent area of the hills should be covered by the forests. During the last 44 years of planning, stress was laid to bring more area under forests, but the achievements in this respect was not upto the expectation. Moreover, with the increase in the size of population along with increased pressure on forest land, about 45 lakh hectares of forest land has been lost to agriculture, industrial estates, river valley projects, transportation projects and different other uses during the last 35 years.

This sort of continues large-scale deforestation is directly responsible for soil erosion, greater frequency and intensity of floods, continuous heavy siltation of costly dams and river banks, change in climate conditions and ecological imbalance. Moreover, deforestation has resulted huge suffering to landless cultivators and marginal farmers in the form of loss of fuel, wood and fodder for their cattle. This in turn is responsible for loss of valuable organic manure as cow-dung is now-a-days largely being used as fuel. Thus deforestation has created both ecological and socio-economic problems in the country.

Since the forest is the "Green Gold" of our country, it must be protected by various forest regulation Act. Until and unless the alarming growth rate of population has not been controlled our Socio-economic progress would be impossible.

The various unknown diseases like AIDS, Cancers, T.B. and other uncurable diseases are the recurring phenomenon due to the environmental pollution. Therefore, I would like to conclude my speech India should limit her size of population.

References

Dutt & Sundaram, *Indian Economy.*

Mishra & Puri, *Indian Economy.*

P.K. Dhar, *Indian Economy its Growing Dimensions.*

B.C. Parida and Dr. Saroj Kumar Kanungo, *Indian Economy.*

Pratiyogita Darpan, 1999.

Kurukshetra, Oct. 1993.

8

Growth of Population and Economic Development of Puri District of Orissa

— *B.N. Dalai & R.N. Misra*

The growth of population has close relationship with the natural resources. The population growth and their characteristics provide a fundamental basis for the evaluation of socio-economic situation in a region. It is now realized that demographic measures are among key factors in the planning process for socio-economic development. The size, structure and distribution of population are essential for any plant that involves food, housing, education, health and other public health services. Population of underdeveloped part is increasing at a very fast rate because the death rate has been reduced and the birth rate continues at its high level. Population is changing the natural and cultural environment to improve the standard of living. The socio-economic development has been outstripped by unprecedented growth of population, therefore, the living standard of population is declining significantly. The unplanned growth of population is mainly responsible for shortage of food, water, house and various other socio-economic amenities (Khosla, 1976: 53). In the study region population is increasing at a very fast rate and therefore its pressure on natural and socio-economic resources is also increasing continuously. The persistence of poverty remains the basic socio-economic problem and a major challenge for development policy. The steps are being taken to curb the growth of population. In India family planning programme has been taken up on a national basis by the Government to control the population. The Government of India has accorded high priority to the family planning programme for the purpose of stabilising the growth of population over a reasonable period, in order to achieve the overall objective of balanced economic and social development. The family planning programme has been in existence for about four decades. Obviously, it has had it ups and downs during this period. The evaluation of the programme after every decade or so, as stated earlier, could help in the assessment of what is being done and to find out as to what could be done further to make the programme conform to the changing requirements. The period of the seventies has been crucial from this angle as this period witnessed notable achievements as well as divergent policy directives which were naturally expected to have significant impact during the eighties and beyond.

Demographic Scenario

Puri District is one of the most densely populated district of the state. The trend of growth of population is seen from table-1.

The table 1 indicates that the district has a total population of 35.90 lakhs according to 1991 census which constitutes 11.33 per cent of the total population ot the state. The decadal growth rate of population indicates that the district had a growth rate of population of about 22.90 per cent between 1981 and 1991 as against the State average

Table 1

Trend of Growth of Population in Puri District and Orissa: 1971, 1981 & 1991

Year	*Population in Puri District*	*Decadal growth rate in Puri District*	*Density of population per sq.km. in Puri District*	*Percentage of district population to the State total*	*Population in Orissa*	*Decadal growth rate of population in Orissa*	*Density of population per sq.km. in Orissa*
1	2	3	4	5	6	7	8
1971	23.40	24.79	230	10.66	219.44	25.05	141
1981	29.21	24.39	287	11.07	263.07	20.17	169
1991	35.90	22.90	385	11.33	316.60	20.06	203

Source: Government of Orissa, D.S. & E., *Statistical Abstract of Orissa* (1981, 1995), Bhubaneswar.

Government of Orissa, D.S. & E., *Economic Survey of Orissa*, (1995-96), Bhubaneswar.

of 22.06 per cent during the said period. Similarly in the earlier decade (i.e., 1971-1981 and 1961-1971) the district had 24.39 per cent and 24.79 per cent growth rates of population as against the state average of 20.17 per cent and 25.05 per cent respectively during the aforesaid decades. Over the decades, although growth rate of population in the district had declined yet it still accounts for a sizable proportion. It is further seen that the average annual growth rate of population during the decade 1981-91 stood at 2.2 per cent. The same was 2.4 per cent during the decade 1971-81. Inspite of the decline in the annual growth rate of population, the burden of population in the district appears to be high.

The heavy concentration of population in the district is further strengthened by the fact that average density per square kilometre was 385 in 1991 as against 287 and 230 persons per sq. kilometre in 1981 and 1971 respectively. It is seen that the density per square kilometre in Puri district was higher than the state average of 203 in 1991. The same sort of situation was also noticed in the preceding census decades.

Male and Female

Furthermore, out of the total population of the district in 1991, the male population was found to be more than female population. This is seen from the table 2. The table indicates that in 1991, the share of male population in the total was 18.51 lakhs. On the other hand the share of female population in the total was 17.39 lakhs, percentage-wise the male population constituted 51.56 per cent, and the female population accounted for 18.44 per cent of the total. In the preceeding decades too males dominated over females in the total composition of population. Accordingly, the sex ratio shows that there were 940 females for 1000

Table 2

Male and Female Distribution of Population in Puri District & Orissa: 1971, 1981 & 1991.

(in lakhs)

Year	*PURI*				*ORISSA*			
	Total Population	*Male*	*Female*	*Sex Ratio (Female per 1000 males)*	*Total population*	*Male*	*Female*	*Sex Ratio (Female per 1000 males)*
1	2	3	4	5	6	7	8	9
1971	23.40	11.83	11.57	977	219.44	110.41	109.03	988
1981	29.21	14.90	14.31	960	263.70	132.53	131.17	982
1991	35.90	18.51	17.39	940	316.60	160.64	155.96	971

Source: Government of Orissa, D.S. & E., *Statistical Abstract of Orissa*, (1981, 1995), Bhubaneswar.
Government of Orissa, D.S. & E., *Economic Survey of Orissa*, (1995-96), Bhubaneswar.

Table 3

Rural and Urban Distribution of Population in Puri & Orissa : 1971, 1981, 1991.

(in lakhs)

Year	*PURI*			*ORISSA*		
	Rural population	*Urban population*	*Total population*	*Rural population*	*Urban population*	*Total population*
1	2	3	4	5	6	7
1971	21.11	2.29	23.40	200.99	18.45	219. 44
	(90.21)	(9.79)	(100.00)	(91.59)	(8.41)	(100.00)
1981	24.89	4.32	29.21	232.59	31.11	263.70
	(85.21)	(14.79)	(100.00)	(88.20)	(11.800)	(100.00)
1991	28.84	7.06	35.90	274.24	42.36	316.60
	(80.330)	(19.670)	(100.00)	(86.620)	(13.380)	(100.00)

Source : Government of Orissa, D.S. & E., *Statistical Abstract of Orissa*, (1981, 1995), Bhubaneswar.
Government of Orissa, D.S. & E., *Economic Survey of Orissa*, (1995-96), Bhubaneswar.

Table 4

Distribution of Population by Literacy in Puri District

Year	*Total population*	*Total Life-rate*	*Male*	*Female*	*Rural*	*Urban*	*% of Life rate to Total*
1	2	3	4	5	6	7	8
1971	23.40	8.28	5.90	2.38			35.3
		(35.3)	(71.26)	(28.74)			
1981	29.21	13.29	8.83	4.46	10.54	2.75	45.5
		(45.5)	(66.44)	(33.56)	(42.35)	(63.65)	
1991	35.90	19.40	12.00	7.40	14.57	4.83	54.3
		(54.3)	(61.9)	(38.10)	(50.8)	(68.4)	

Source: Government of Orissa, D.S. & E., *Statistical Abstract of Orissa,* (1981, 1995), Bhubaneswar.

Government of Orissa, D.S. & E., *Economic Survey of Orissa,* (1995-96), Bhubaneswar.

males in 1991. In the earlier decade (i.e., 1981) the sex ratio was 960 females for 1000 males. Sex ratio thus indicates a bias towards males than females in Puri District.

Rural and Urban

Like the state, the district is more rural than urban. According to 1991 census, merely 87.0 per cent of the state's population lived in rural areas. In the earlier decades (i.e., 1971 and 1981) the percentage share of rural population to the total in the district was 90.21 per cent and 85.21 per cent respectively. Over the years, although the percentage share of the rural population to the total in the district declined, yet the rural population still constituted a larger segment of the total. The apparent decline in rural population to the districts total is due to the concommittent growth of urban population during the said years. It is observed from (Table 3) that in 1971 the share of urban population to the total in the district stood at 9.79 per cent. The same was 14.79 per cent in 1981. This further increased to 19.67 in 1991. This growth of urban population is an indication of the move towards urbanisation which has occurred in the recent past.

Caste-wise Population

The caste-wise distribution of population as shown in Table 5 reveals that the district has more of scheduled caste population than scheduled tribes. According to 1991 census the share of SC population stood at 15.45 per cent, whereas ST population was only 3.53 per cent of the total. Out of the total SC and ST population of the state, the share of Puri district was 5.61 per cent in 1991. In the earlier census decades. too, one notices the percentage where SC population being more than the ST population to the total. Since SC and ST population constitute the most vulnerable

Table 5

Caste-wise Distribution of Population in Puri & Orissa (1971, 1981 & 1991)

Year	*PURI*			*ORISSA*		
	SC Population	*ST Population*	*Total Population*	*SC Population*	*ST Population*	*Total Population*
1	2	3	4	5	6	7
1971	3.17	0.87	23.40	33.10	50.71	219.44
	(13.54)	(3.70)	(100.00)	(15.08)	(23.10)	(100.00)
1981	3.77	1.00	29.21	38.65	59.15	263.70
	(12.9)	(3.42)	(100.00)	(14.65)	(22.43)	(100.00)
1991	5.55	1.27	35.90	51.29	70.32	316.00
	(15.450)	(3.53)	(100.00)	(16.20)	(22.21)	(100.00)

Source: Government of Orissa, D.S. & E., *Statistical Abstract of Orissa,* (1981, 1995), Bhubaneswar.

Government of Orissa, D.S. & E., *Economic Survey of Orissa,* (1995-96), Bhubaneswar.

sections of the community in the district, efforts have been made for their rehabilitation by creating suitable employment opportunities both in farm and non-farm sectors.

Literacy

Distribution of population by literacy shows that the district has performed well in this field. Table 4 indicates that the literacy rate of the district was 54.3 per cent as against the state average of 49.09 per cent in 1991. Among the literate population, male literate accounted for 61.9 per cent of the total. On the other hand, female literates constituted about 38.1 per cent of the total population in the district. This was also true in the preceding census decades. A further look into rural and urban literate population in the district indicates that the percentage share of urban literates to the total was higher than the rural literates. According to 1991 census, the percentage share of urban literates to total population stood at 68.4. The same was 50.8 for the rural literates. The corresponding figures for 1981 was 63.65 per cent and 42.35 per cent respectively. The higher urban literacy is due to the spread of large number of educational institutions in the district and the presence of state capital in the district.

Occupational Structure

The occupational distribution of population reveals that bulk of the population in the district depend upon agriculture for their livelihood and occupation. The available data (Table 6) reveal that in 1991 nearly 65.0 per cent of workers consisting of cultivators and agricultural labourers depended solely on agriculture and allied activities for employment, On the other hand, workers engaged in household and other industrial activities accounted for only 6.93 per cent of the total. In the earlier census decades (i.e., 1971 and 1981) workers depended upon agriculture and activities accounted for 72.16 per cent and 67.56 per cent respectively of the total. Likewise workers engaged in industrial occupations constituted 3.53 per cent and 3.38 per cent respectively at the total in 1971 and 1981. It is noticed that over the census decades, percentage share of workers depending on agriculture and allied activities and handicraft units had declined. This decline was more due to the expansion of tertiary activities consisting of trade and business and other service sectors. The data reveals that workers engaged in tertiary sector stood at 8.74 per cent of the total workers in 1991. Inspite of the expansion of service sector in the district agriculture still continues to be the principal sector of the economy. In this context therefore, development of agro-industries is mooted to provide employment facilities of surplus agricultural population whose marginal productivity is low.

Conclusions

1. Concepts of population education should be introduced at all levels of education, primary, secondary and higher education. In view of the paucity of resources for school buildings and equipment, we should further explore the possibility of using mass media (including the establishing of more T.V. stations, and radio schools on the lines of the highly successful sutatenza experiment in Colombia, South America) for population education.

2. To avoid increasing the financial burden by introducing additional courses, population education should be integrated with all subjects. The existing syllabi for social and biological sciences

should be reoriented to focus attention on human development in the context of high population growth.

3. The emphasis in the curriculum should be not only on the mechanics or the facts of life and the causes of population growth, but on values, such as human dignity, self respect and responsible parenthood.
4. Population education should be integrated into functional literacy and social education programmes including premarital counselling for adults and out of school youth. This could be made conditional to marriage registration.
5. In order to increase the effectiveness of population education programmes, there is an urgent need for teachers and social workers to be given an intensive course on population education. These topics could be incorporated in the training colleges preparing elementary and secondary school teachers. Short term programmes of a duration of 8 to 10 days could be introduced for teachers, parents and social workers.

References

Barnabas, A.P. (1977). *Population Control in India (Policy Administration Spread)*, IIPA, New Delhi, pp. 12-15.

Bhargava, M. and Khajuria (1990). "A comparative Study of Health Distress and the Behaviour/Attitudes of Family Planning Adopters and Non-adopters." *The Journal of Family Welfare*, Vol. 36, No. 2, pp. 3-20.

Bhogle, S. and Kaur, S. (1972). *Adoption of Family Planning in Two Industrial Settings—A comparative study*. Council for Social Development, New Delhi.

Das, N. (1972). "Factor relate to knowledge. Family Size Preference and Practice of Family Planning in India." *The Journal of Family Planning,* Vol. 19, No.1, Sept. pp. 40-52.

Gupta, Pullikal and Kothari (1991). "Women's participation of time in rural India: Possible Implication for Family Welfare programme." *The Journal of Family Planning,* Vol. 37, No. 1, pp. 42-98.

Gopal Rao Kamla (1974). *Studies in Family Planning in India,* Abhinav Publications, New Delhi, pp. 863.

The World Bank, *World Development Report—1984,* Oxford University Press, 1984. p.11.

UNDP Human Development Report. Oxford University Press, New York, 1990, pp. 1-7.

9
Demography of the Matia Community—A Study

—N.C. Dash & S.K. Sahu

Matia, a sub-division of the Gonds, is one of the aboriginal tribes of Andhra Pradesh. In course of time they have migrated to Orissa. They are widely distributed in Orissa except Kalahandi district. Matias count 12,124 in number according to 1981 census, (Census of India 1981). In 2001 the estimated population of Matia community is 16,861. The term 'Matia' means soil. As these people are specialised in earth work (Soil digging) they are called as 'Matia.' The tribe Matia is also called as 'Mattiya' (Thurston and Rangachari 1993). Their mother tongue is Telugu but they fluently speak Oriya as those of the local people.

In the present study, an attempt has been made to highlight the demographic scenario of Matia tribes in Orissa.

The sample Matia village, Madanmohanpur is situated at a distance of 11 kilometres south-west of Berhampur city. The study was conducted in the entire village by canvassing three structured schedules: (1) Household census schedule, (2) Marriage and fertility schedule, and (3) Schedule for mortality. Interview technique was mainly

Table 1

Distribution of Population by Household Size

Household Size	1	2	3	4	5	6	7	8	9	10	Total
Distribution of Household	06 (5.45)	12 (10.91)	20 (18.18)	24 (21.82)	20 (18.18)	14 (12.73)	07 (6.36)	03 (2.73)	03 (2.73)	01 (0.91)	110 (100)
Total Population	06	24	60	96	100	84	49	24	27	10	480

(Average Household size: 4.36)

adopted for filling in the schedules. Observation technique, particularly, non-participant type was also followed as should be for any empirical study. Data has been collected from 110 households during December 1999.

Family Size and Composition

As large as 110 Matia households have been covered in this survey. The family (Household) size is defined as the number of persons who reside under one roof and share food from single kitchen.

The Table 1 depicts the distribution of Matia population by the size of the households. The average household size is 4.36. It is also found from the above data that maximum distribution (21.82%) is noticed in the 4 member households and the lowest distribution (0.91%) is found in 10 member households. Interestingly 3 and 5 members families are equally distributed 18.18% each. The village consists of 110 households with a total population of 480 individuals.

Population Structure

Age and sex structure of the population is very much important for every socio-economic study. The age and sex composition of the Matia village is presented in Table 2.

The table 2 depicts that the distribution of Matia males and females in the total population, are 51.87% and 48.13% respectively. The mean age of males is 27.58 and that of the female is 26.14 years. Interestingly the male mean age is more than the females. The sex ratio is 928 females per 1000 males, which is at par with the national sex ratio. The proportion of child population, economic active population and aged population are 33.3 per cent, 58.75 per cent and 7.9 per cent respectively. The sex ratio favours the females in the economic active age group i.e. 1254 females per 1000 males. But in child and aged age groups, the sex ratio

Table 2

Distribution of Population by Age and Sex

Age Group	*Male*	*Percentage*	*Female*	*Percentage*	*Total*	*Percentage*
0-4	22	4.58	22	4.58	44	9.17
5-9	32	6.67	28	5.83	60	12.50
10-14	31	6.46	25	5.21	56	11.67
15-19	25	5.21	30	6.25	55	11.45
20-24	21	4.39	23	4.80	44	9.17
25-29	22	4.58	16	3.93	38	7.91
30-34	12	2.50	16	3.33	28	5.83
35-39	15	3.12	12	2.50	27	5.62
40-44	11	2.30	18	3.75	29	6.04
45-49	15	3.12	14	2.92	29	6.04
50-54	12	2.50	08	1.67	20	4.17
55-59	06	1.25	06	1.25	12	2.50
60+	25	5.21	13	2.71	38	7.91
Total	249	51.87	231	48.13	480	100.00

(Median Age: Male-27.58, Female-26.14)

favours males i.e 882 and 520 females respectively per 1000 males. The low male sex ratio in the eco-active age group indicates that the males are out of the village in search of their livelihood. The low female sex ratio in the aged group suggests that the longevity of the females is low compared to their male counterparts.

Dependency Ratio

The dependency of population is based on the fact that every member of the society is a consumer and only few members are producers, (Thompson and Lewis, 1965). The dependency ratios have been calculated in relation to the economic active age group 15-59 years. The distribution of economic active age group and dependency ratio are presented in Table 3.

The child and aged dependency ratio among the Matia are 0.57 and 0.13 respectively. The total dependency ratio of Matias is 0.70 per one economic active individual. The lower dependency is marked due to higher distribution of population in the economic active age group.

Table 3

Distribution of Population by Broad Age Groups and Dependency Ratio

Age Group	*Population*	*Percentage*	*Types of Dependency*	*Dependency Ratio*
0-14	160	33.33%	Child Dependency (0.14/15-59)	0.57
15-59	282	58.75	Productive group	
60+	38	7.92%	Aged dependency (60+/ 15-59)	0.13
Total	480	(100)	Total Dependency (0-14 + 60+/15-59)	0.70

Educational Standards

Educational standard of a community determines the economic status, Table 4 depicts that the total literacy ratio of Matias is 46 per cent whereas the total literates in the state is 49 per cent. It is evident from the table that the Matias are not far away from the main stream. It is all possible because there is a permanent school in the village. The higher distributions of literates in the younger age group suggests increasing interest for education among the younger generation.

Table 4

Distribution of Population by Educational Standard

Age	*Illiterate*		*Upto 5th class*		*Upto 7th class*		*Upto 10th class*		*Above 10th Class*		*Total Literate*		*Grand Total*	
Group.	*M*	*F*	*M*	*F*	*M*	*F*	*M*	*F*	*M*	*F*	*M*	*F*	*M*	*F*
5-14	20	23	35	29	08	01	...	...	...	...	43	30	63	53
15-24	02	40	08	05	12	02	22	06	02	...	44	13	46	53
25-34	06	26	09	05	09	...	09	01	01	...	28	06	34	32
35-44	06	27	09	03	06	...	05	...	...	....	20	03	26	30
45-54	19	20	05	02	02	...	01	...	...	...	08	02	27	22
55+	27	19	04	...	...	...	...	...	...	...	04		31	19
Total	80 (35.2)	155 (74.16)	70 (30.8)	44 (21.1)	37 (16.2)	03 (1.4)	37 (16.2)	07 (3..3)	03 (1.3)	... ...	147 (64.75)	54 (25.8)	221 (100)	209 (100)

(Population below 5 years are excluded)

Further, the table reveals that the proportion of illiterates is as high as 74 per cent among females and 35 per cent among males. The total literate among males is 65 per cent and that of the female is 26 per cent whereas the total literate in Orissa is 63 per cent for males and 35 per cent for females. This indicates that Matia males are quite advanced in literacy in comparison to total male literacy of the State. However, there are only 1.3 per cent of males who have studied above standard ten in the entire village. This shows that the higher education is yet to be achieved. This would be possible if the present younger generation continues their studies without further dropouts.

Occupational Pattern

The occupational pattern of the economic active Matia is shown in the following table. The main occupation of Matia is wage earning and Government service, Table 5.

Table 5

Distribution of Economic Active Population by Primary and Secondary Occupation

Name of the Occupation	*Male*	*Percentage*	*Female*	*Percentage*	*Total*	*Percentage*
Agriculture	11	(07.91)	09	(06.29)	20	(07.09
Wage earner	76	(54.67)	99	(69.23)	175	(62.03)
Govt. service	33	(23.74)	03	(02.09)	36	(12.76)
N.G.O.	03	(02.15)	...	...	03	(01.06)
Mat Makers	...	...	08	(05.59)	08	(02.83)
Buffalo Rearing	07	(05.03)	09	(06.29)	16	(05.67)
Rickshaw Puller	03	(02.15)	...	...	03	(01.06)
Small Business	03	(02.15)	...	...	03	(01.06)
Total workers	136	(97.84)	128	(89.51)	264	(93.61)
Total Non-worker	03	(02.15)	15	(10.48)	018	(06.38)
Grand Total	139	(100)	143	(100)	282	(100)

The table reveals that 54..67per cent males and 69.23 females are wage earners. Besides these traditional occupation, i.e. digging soil (earth work), the Matias are engaged in different economic activities such as agriculture, Govt. & Non-Govt. service, mat making, buffalo rearing, rickshaw pulling, N.G.O. service and small business. The above table reveals that as large as 7.91 per cent males and 6.29 per cent females are engaged in agriculture, 23.74 per cents males and 2.09 per cent females engaged in Govt. & Non-Govt. service As large as 2.15 per cent and 5.59 per cent females are engaged in Non-Govt. Sector and mat making respectively. More than 5 per cent males and 6 per cent females are engaged in buffalo rearing. A total of 2.15 per cent male active population are engaged in rickshaw pulling and interestingly the same percentage of males are engaged in small business.

Income and Expenditure

The total income and expenditure of the family from different sources have been calculated and categorised by monthly basis. The Table 6 and Table 7 reveal the income and expenditure of the Matias.

The figure in the table shows the maximum number of families (26) earn in the range of Rs. 1501/- to 2000/- per month. There are 25 families earn Rs. 1000/- and below only 3 families earn above Rs. 5000/-. Thus the average monthly income of the Matia is Rs. 1788/- per family. This shows that the Matias are slightly above the poverty line of the state i.e. Rs. 1300/- per family per month.

The data in the table 7 depicts the maximum 30 number of families spend in the range of Rs. 1501/- to 2000/- per month. There are 27 families who spend Rs. 1000/- and below. Only 2 families spend in the range of Rs. 4001/- to 5000/- per month. The average monthly expenditure of

Table 6

Distribution of Monthly Income by Family Size

Family Income	*Family Size*										*Total*
	1	*2*	*3*	*4*	*5*	*6*	*7*	*8*	*9*	*10*	
Below -1000	6	8	8	3	...	...	...	...	...	...	25
1001-1500.	..	3	5	5	2	4	3	...	...	...	22
1501-2000		5	8	8	3	1	...	...	...	...	26
2001-2500	...	...	2	6	5	3	...	...	...	...	16
2501-3000	...	....	...	1	3	2	1	....	...	...	08
3001-3500	...	...	...	1	2	1	1	...	...	...	05
3501-4000	...	...	...	...	...	...	1	1	....	...	02
4001-4500	...	..	...	...	...	...	...	1	...	...	01
4501-5000	...	...	...	...	...	...	...	1	1	...	02
5000 & above	...	...	...	..	..	...	...	...	2	1	03
Total	6	12	20	24	20	14	7	3	3	1	110

(Average monthly income is Rs. 1788/- per family)

Table 7

Distribution of Monthly Expenditure by Family Size.

Family Expenditure	*Family Size*										*Total*
	1	*2*	*3*	*4*	*5*	*6*	*7*	*8*	*9*	*10*	
Below -1000	6	7	9	5	...	...	...	...	...	...	27
1001-1500	...	3	5	9	4	3	...	...	...	...	24
1501-2000	...	2	6	9	8	3	2	...	...	...	30
2001-2500	...	..	...	1	7	6	...	...	...	...	14
2501-3000	...	...	...	...	1	2	2	1	...	...	06
3001-3500	...	...	...	...	...	...	2	1	1	...	04
3501-4000	...	...	...	...	...	...	1	1	1	...	03
4001-4500	...	...	...	...	...	...	...	...	1	...	01
4501-5000	...	...	...	...	...	...	...	...	...	1	01
5000 & above	...	...	...	...	...	...	...	...	...	...	...
Total	6	12	20	24	20	14	7	3	3	1	110

(Average monthly expenditure is Rs. 1611/- per family)

the Matias is Rs. 1611/- per family. Considering their family income and expenditure it could be said that the Matias must be saving around Rs. 200/- per month for their emergencies.

Marital Status

Marriage is a social institution and has its own importance in Matia society. The marital status provides the basic information regarding the vulnerable group responsible for fertility. The data in Table 8 on next page reveals the marital status of the Matia community.

It is interesting to note from the table 8 that no marriages below 15 years of age are practised among Matias at present. There are nearly 45 per cent Matia males and 42 per cent females are unmarried. About 46 per cent Matia males and 50 per cent females get currently married. The widowed males and females constitute as large as 4 per cent and 7 per cent respectively. The corresponding figure for divorced/separated males and females constitute very negligible.

This indicates that widowed, divorced and separated males remarry compared to females. Matia status of the reproductive women shows that about 50.2 per cent of the fecund women are currently married, 9.5 per cent are unmarried and the rest are widowed, divorced and separated 7.8 per cent.

Age at Marriage

Age at marriage being a socio-cultural factor has an important role in the demographic studies. The average age at first marriage of the Matia is 17.65 years for the females and 22.89 years for the males.The age at first marriage among the Matias is depicted in Table 9.

Table 8

Distribution of Population by Marital Status and Age.

Age Group	*Unmarried*		*Married*		*Marital Status* *Widowed*		*Div/Sep*		*Ever Married*		*Total*	
	M	*F*	*M*	*F*	*M*	*F*	*M*	*F*	*M*	*F*	*M*	*F*
Below 15	85	75	..	..	..	...	...	...	...	...	85	75
15-19	25	18	...	12	...	...	...	...	...	12	25	30
20-24	10	04	11	19	...	...	...	...	11	19	21	23
25-29	02	...	20	16	...	...	...	...	20	16	22	16
30-34	...	...	12	14	...	...	...	01	12	16	12	16
35-39	...	...	14	11	...	01	01	...	15	12	15	12
40-44	...	...	11	16	...	02	...	..	11	18	11	18
45-49	...	...	15	13	...	01	...	...	15	14	15	14
50 +	...	...	33	15	10	12	...	...	43	27	43	27
Total	122 (49%)	97 (42%)	116 (46.58)	116 (50.21	10 (4.01)	17 (7.36)	1 (0.40)	1 (0.43)	127 (51)	134 (58)	249 (100)	231 (100)

Table 9

Distribution of Ever Married Population by Age at First Marriage.

Present Age	*Age at First Marriage* *Below-15*		*15-19*		*20-24*		*25-29*		*30+*		*Total*	
	M	*F*	*M*	*F*	*M*	*F*	*M*	*F*	*M*	*F*	*M*	*F*
Below 15	...	...	...	...	...	...	...	...	...	...	...	...
15-19	...	...	...	12	...	...	...	...	...	...	...	12
20-24	...	...	...	16	9	3	2	...	...	...	11	19
25-29	...	...	...	10	11	6	9	...	...	...	20	16
30-34	...	...	...	09	08	07	02	...	02	...	12	16
35-39	...	01	...	09	09	02	04	...	02	...	15	12
40-44	01	03	01	13	05	01	03	01	01	...	11	18
45-49	01	05	02	08	08	01	04	...	...	...	15	14
50+	03	12	17	12	17	03	06	...	...	...	43	27
Total	05	21	20	89	67	23	30	01	05	...	127	134
	(3.9)	(15.6)	(15.7)	(66.4)	(52.7)	(17.1)	23.6)	(0.7)	(3.9)	...	(100)	(100)

(Average age at first marriage male 22.89 yrs. and female 17.65 yrs.)

The table 9 clearly shows that maximum numbers of Matia females marry between 15-19 years of age (66.4) per cent and maximum numbers of males marry between 20-24 years of age (52.7) per cent. Almost all females prefer to marry before 25 years of age and that of males before 30 years of age. Marriages below 15 years of age are found among the Matia males and females in higher age groups. It indicates child marriages are not marked during last two decades.

Fertility Analysis

(Fertility is the process through which addition or replacement is brought in a population by both fertility refers to the actual occurrence of birth especially the live births (Cox 1969). For various measurements of fertility, the age specific rates of the women, in different age groups are very much essential.) The distributions of age specific rate among the Matias have been presented in Table 10.

Table 10

Age Specific Fertility Rate

Fecund Age group	*Women of that age group*	*Currently Married women*	*Children born last year*			*A.S.F.R*	*ASMFR*
			M	*F*	*T*		
15-19	30	12	2	1	3	0.10	0.25
20-24	23	19	4	3	7	0.30	0.37
25-29	16	16	1	2	3	0.18	0.18
30.34	16	14	1	...	1	0.06	0.07
35-39	12	11	...	...	...	...	...
40-44	18	16	...	...	...	...	...
Total	115	88	8	6	14	0.64	0.87

(TFR): 0.64 x class interval) = .64 x 5 = 3.20

(TFM): 0.87 x class interval) =.87 x 5 = 4.35

The total live births are 14 out of which 8 are male and 6 are female children. Maximum numbers of children are born by the women in the age group of 20-24 years during the survey period.

Measurement of Fertility

There are several measurement of births to establish the native and trend of fertility. The crude birth rate (C.B.R) of the Matias during the period is 29 per 1000 population. The general fertility rate (G.F.R.) and general marital fertility rate (G.M.F.R.) are 121 and 159 per 1000 females respectively. The total fertility rate (T.F.R.) and total marital fertility rate (T.M.F.R.) of the population is found to be 3.20 and 4.35 respectively. The child woman ratio (C.W.R) of the Matia population during the survey period is 338 per 1000 females (Children below 5 years to women 15-49 yrs.). All the fertility measurements indicate that the Matias have a lower schedule of fertility compared to those of the State figures.

Mortality Analysis

Mortality means the measurement of deaths in the population. It is another important factor, which determines the size of population. It also influences the composition of the population different age groups among the Matias are shown in Table 11.

The table-11 shows that male deaths are more than that of the female i.e. 57.1 per cent and 42.9 per cent respectively. Last year there is only one infant death in this village. The crude death rate (CDR) of Matia is 14.58. Interestingly the mortality rates are more or less similar to the corresponding figures of the State.

Table 11

Distribution of Death by Age & Sex

Specific Age Group	*Number of deaths during last year* *Male*	*Female*	*Total*
00-01	-1 (14.3)	...	1-(14.3)
01-14	...	...	...
15-44	...	02(28.6)	02(28.6)
45-49	1 (14.3)	.....	1 (14.3)
50-59	1 (14.3)	...	1(14.3)
60+	1 (14.3)	1(14.3)	2 (28.6)
Total	4(57.1)	3 (42.9)	7(100)

(Figures in brackets show percentage).

Summary

The mean age of population is, male 27.5 and female 26.1 years. The economic active population is 46 per cent. The aged and child population are 8 per cent and 33 per cent respectively. The sex ratio is 928 females per 1000 males.

The proportion of literate among Matia males is about 65 per cent and females is 26 per cent. Wage earnings particularly earthwork, is the main occupation of the the Matias. Nearly 54 per cent males and 69 per cent females are engaged in wage earning. Only about 8 per cent males and 6 per cent females are engaged in agricultural sector.

It is interesting to note that marriages below 15 years of age are not practised at present. The average age at first marriage of Matia male is about 23 years and female is 18 years which are almost similar to the government recommended age. The average monthly family income is Rs. 1788/- and average monthly expenditure is Rs. 1611/-

The surplus income indicate that the Matias are happy with their present income pattern, although this is slightly above the poverty line.

The birth rate of Matias is 29 per 1000 population and the total fertility rate (TFR) among the Matia is 3.2 per cent. The death rate of the Matia is 14 per 1000 population. The birth and death schedule of the Matia community is about similar to the State figures.

The Matia although a semi nomadic tribe need thoughtful care by the Government and Nongovernment organisations for their all-round development which will bring peace and bliss in the Matia community of Orissa.

References

Barclay, W.G. (1958). *Techniques of Population Analysis*, New York.

Census of India (1981). *General Population and Population of Scheduled Tribes and Castes*, Paper-1 of 1984.

Cox, P.R. (1969). *Demography*, Cambridge University Press.

Rangachari, K. and Thurston, E. (1993) *Caste and Tribes of Southern India*, Vol. 5, pp. 49-51.

Thomson, W.S. and Lewis, D.T. (1965). *Population Problems*, New York.

10
Effects of Population and Indian Economy

—Premananda Pradhan

The 1991 census has starkingly highlighted the consequences of the overall failure of our F.P. Programme in terms of regulating the "Population explosion. India today possesses about 2.4 per cent of the total land area of the World but she has to support about 16 per cent of the World population. Populationwise India stands second in the World after China. The Table 1 on next page shows India's population in 20th century.

With a population of 846 million as on the sun rise of March 1991 Indian's share in the World population increased to 16 per cent from 15.2 per cent in 1981.

It has been observed that most of the developing countries are passing through the second stage of demographic transition where the death rate falls without a fall in the birth rate. In such a situation, the exploding population hovers over the developing economics like a menacing dark cloud and offsets all their economic prosperity. Economists like Robert Cassen is of the view that "Population Explosion Hinders Economic Development of the Poor Countries as it Compels their Governments to change their Economic Priorities. In such a Context, Feeding the Feeming Millions becomes the First priority of the Government and in the process more important development objectives are neglected."

Table 1

Indian Population in Present Century

Census year	*Population (in crs.)*	*Change per decade (in crs.)*	*Rate of change per decade (%)*	*Compound Average Annual growth rate of population (%)*	*Female-Male Ratio (Females per thousand males*
1891	23.60	-	-	-	-
1901	23.84	+0.24	-	-	972
1911	25.21	+1.37	+5.75	0.56	964
1921	25.13	-0.08	-0.31	-0.03	955
1931	27.90	+2.77	+11.00	1.04	950
1941	31.87	+3.97	+14.22	1.33	945
1951	36.11	+4.24	+13.31	1.25	946
1961	43.92	+7.81	+21.51	1.96	941
1971	54.82	+10.90	+24.80	2.20	930
1981	68.33	+13.51	+24.66	2.22	934
1991	84.63	+16.30	+23.85	2.14	927
1996	93.42*	-	-	-	-

*Economic Survey 1998-99 p S-1.

(1) Social Infrastructure

Rapid growth of population aggravates seriously the problem of pressure in various public utilities and services. High growth of population leads to rush in educational institution, overcrowdness in city transport services, water supply, power supply and traffics. Besides these , there is serious problem of road, transport, power generation, and other infrastructural facilities, because of high growth of population. For instance, there is mounting problem of drainage system and availability of drinking water in urban areas.

(2) Objections of Slum

Due to non-availability of alternative avenues of employment except agriculture in rural areas, people in large scale migrate to urban areas. The rural labour force are generally employed in various fields like earth works, Railways, Roads, Jute Mills, Textile Mills, Brick-klin and other construction works. The large influx of rural labour into urban areas gives birth to various socio-economic problems. The paramount and vital problem is the slum problem. The rural workers inhabits in the road-side pavements in small cottages which are known as slum.

These unorganised, illiterate rural create hygienic problems because of their high concentration in project areas. They are few indulged in anti-social activities, robbery and other social crimes.

3. Degradation of Environment

High growth of population causes multidimensional problems among which environmental problem is considered as an important one.

Due to high growth of population there is high demand for certain basic amenities of life. Those are house, cloth and shelter. For building houses, there is not only requirements of stones, bricks but also fire wood and timber. Thus, it has a direct link on the forest resources of the country. Because by cutting trees various types of equipments like door, window, furniture etc. are constructed. Even for making bricks fire-wood is used. Though the proportion of forest areas depletes lead to environmental and ecological problems.

The rainwater falling on the top hill of the forest is not of abstracted due to depletion of forest. It washes the fertile soil causing soil-erosion and swells the river beds. Ultimately, floods and due to erratic monsoon droughts are becoming recuring phenomenon.

High growth of population leads to excess demand for industrial products. As a result, there is stupendous growth of industries. This industrialisation emit paismeous gasses to the surface polluting the air. The wastages are left through drains to rivers which is detrimental not only to mankind but also to fish and other living creatures.

4. Obstacle to Capital Formation

In underdeveloped countries savings are low and capital requirements are great. When the size of the family is large, consumption expenditure will reduce the volume of savings. Moreover, in underdeveloped countries, majority of the people live at a subsistance level. Their propensity to consume is high. When their income rise, their consumption also rises. As a result consumption expenditure increases and Savings decreases. When the volume of savings is low, the rate of investment will become low. The result is, low capital formation does not lead to rapid economic development of the country.

5. Unemployment

Rapidly rising population is aggravating the unemployment problem in the country. Creating large scale un-employment in the urban areas as well as a huge extent of disguised unemployment in the rural areas. At the end of each five year plan the back log of unemployment in India is increasing as the volume of employment generated could not match this additional member of labour included in work force. As per the document of sixth plan (1980-85) total number of unemployed was 20.7 million in 1980 which represents, 7.74 per cent of total labour force. But the eighth plan (1992-97) has estimated the total backlog of unemployment as 28 million in 1990.

6. *Rising Population and on Productive Consumers*

Excessive growth of population adds the number of unproductive consumer. Their contribution is total productivity is zero, unproductive consumers includes children, old person's and those voluntarily unemployed persons in 15-59 age groups. During the period 1961-81, the ratio of working to non-working population in India has deteriorated from 43:53 per cent in 1961 to 37.6:62.4 per cent in 1981.

7. *Magnitude of Poverty*

Poverty and unemployment are the two most serious problems from which the country has been suffering from the very beginning of the present century. This twin problems of poverty and unemployment have been aggravated in the present century due to increase in population at a high rate and growing inequality in the income distribution. Due to non-availability of employment avenues, a big chunk of the population is deprived of even minimum amenities of life for a long period. The following table high lights relating to number of percentage of population below poverty line.

Number and percentage of population below poverty line: (Number in Million and poverty ratio in %)

	Rural Sector		*Urban Sector*		*India*	
Year	*Numbers in million*	*Poverty ratio*	*Number in million*	*Poverty Ratio*	*Number in Million*	*Poverty Ratio*
1973-74	261	56.4	60	49.0	321	54.9
1977-78	264	53.1	65	45.2	329	51.3
1983-84	252	45.7	71	40.8	323	49.5
1987-88	232	39.1	75	38.2	307	38.9
1993-94	244	37.3	76	32.4	320	36.0

Source: Economic Survey 1998-99 (p-146)

Suggestions

1. The mass Media have to continue to play their role for increasing the awareness and creating a climate for the acceptance of the programme. But it is direct to change the attitude of the people. That role has to be played by the people themselves, by voluntary organisations, and the opinion leaders on whom the farmers and landless labourers rely for advice and help.
2. Thirdly, very high monetary reward may be offered for sterilisation after one child and little lower after two children and much lower after three. Such families are sending their girls to school may be provided employment for their unemployed adults on a preferential basis.
3. Gram Panchayats can play a vital role in mobilising the village people to actively participate in educating and motivating the people to accept family planning. Distribution of good quality contraceptives can be better maintained by Mahila Mandalas in the village areas. In rural areas, still a large proportion of

deliveries are conducted by untrained *dais*. These dais can be trained in conducting the deliveries and, at the same time, their contacts with all women in villages can be utilised for spreading the message of family planning as well as services.

4. Moreover a good number of contraceptive distribution centres should be established both in the urban as well as rural areas of the country. These contraceptives should be supplied to married couples after providing knowledge and purpose.
5. Elementary education to be made free and compulsory. Further, Registration of marriage, to be made compulsory along with births and deaths.
6. Priority in the family planning programmes should be given on educating women about the techniques of family planning and inculcating in them the conviction and resolve to limiting the family. Education of women is of paramount importance for the progress of any state in the country. For example Kerala.

To conclude, Rapid population growth in India has created gigantic problems which are manifested in political, social, economic environmental and psychological upheavals that are frequently occurring all over the country. Population problem is the central problem in which all other problems revolving to it. No doubt, improving in the literacy levels of the people would be definitely fruitful and would bring down the rate of population growth.

References

P.K. Dhar, *Indian Economy, It's growing dimensions* (Kalyani Publisher), 2000.

Pratiyogita Darpana, June 2000.

Economic Survey- 1998-99 (p. 146)

Dr. Kamta Prasad, Policy options for stabilising rural Population. Kurukshetra, October 1993, pp. 22-23.

S.C. Bhatt, "Precious Time Lost: Let's get a more on!" *Kurukshetra*, October, 1993, pp. 30.

11

Stabilising the Population in 21st Century—Human Awareness as the Key-Contraceptive

— R.N. Dalai, G.R. Rao & R.N. Misra

We have stepped into the 21st Century and the first census report of this Century has come out. The 2001 census report reveals that the population of India, second to China, has increased by 1.81 millionduring 1991-2001 decade. It is estimated that we are going to beat China by 2045 if this rate of growth continues. This has caused a serious concern among all the serious thinkers of the nation. An attempt, here has been made to analyse the population data and to introspect the existing as well as the earlier population control measures in order to ascertain where we have missed the bus. Further suitable measures to achieve stabilisation in population growth are also suggested.

Methodology

The relevant population data of India and Orissa from 1951 Census onwards are taken into account for the purpose. The related data of other states have also been used for comparison. Only the simple statistical tools like ratios, rates, percentages have been used for analysing the data.

The population census of India and Orissa since 1951 is exhibited in Table 1.

Table 1

Population of India and Orissa

(in Crores)

Census year	*India Population*	*Increase*	*Growth percentage*	*Orissa Population*	*Increase*	*Growth percentage*
1951	36.11	—	—	1.46	—	—
1961	43.92	7.81	21.63	1.75	0.29	19.86
1971	54.82	10.90	24.82	2.19	0.44	25.14
1981	68.52	13.70	24.99	2.63	0.44	20.17
1991	84.60	16.21	23.46	3.16	0.53	20.06
2001	102.70	17.97	21.34	3.67	0.51	15.94

Source: Compiled from various Census reports of India.

Favourable Aspects of 2001 Census

The Census report of 2001 showed some favourable aspects. An observation of the figure—Table 1 reveals that the population growth rate (PGR) of India has been reduced from 22-86 (during 81-91 Census) to 21-34 showing a decline of 2.52 points. Among all the states the PGR of Kerala is 9.42 which happens to the lowest. Kerala is followed by Tamil Nadu with 11.19 and Andhra Pradesh with 13.86. The decline of PGR in A.P. being 10.34 points which is highest among all the states. In Orissa it has bean reduced from 20.06 (91 Census) to 15.94. A significant decline of 4.52 points is registered.

The reason for the decline in PGR of Kerala, T.N. and A.P. Was due to the gulf factor. For example, in Kerala during 61-71 decade, large number of rural artisans were migrated to gulf countries in search of employment. Thus they not only remained away from their family life but also could earn lot of money. This earning helped them to come under above poverty line within a short span of time This has reduced the PGR of the state since 1971 cansus. The same gulf factor played its role in Tamilnadu and Karnataka and A.P. during the subsequent decade. The overall literacy rate of almost all the states showed a positive growth. It is highest in Kerala with 90.92 per cent. In Orissa 75 per cent males and 54 per cent females are literate.

Unfavourable Aspect of Census Report

Though there are some favourable points. The report has rung a warning bell about the negative aspects. Which need more and more attention. The India's population, second to China, has crossed one billion mark. Even with the reduced PGR, Indian population it is estimated that by 2045 AD could secure first rank, surpassing China. During the 20th Century, the World population became three fold, while it is 5 fold in respect of India. During 1961, every 7th person of the World was an Indian. But now every 6th person is an Indian as about 16.7 per cent population of World live in India. According to some estimates, 3 babies are added for every 5 seconds. At the present PGR, one year is sufficient to produce another Australia and 12 years are enough to add one billion to the World population. If this situation at this rate continuous then one may not get even a milli metre space on land to stand on ones toe. The gravity of the present situation can very well, be imagined from their figures.

Components of Growth of Population

The major components of growth in population figures

are (i) longer life expectancy (ii) low literacy rate and iii) Poverty.

With the improvement in medical and health facilities, over a period of half century, the CDR in India has come down by 27 per thousand to 9 per thousand—representing a reduction of 18 points (66.7 per cent) the CBR too reduced from 40 per thousand to 24 per thousand representing a decline of 16 points (40 per cent). However, the gap between the two rates was 13 during 1951, and 15 during 2001. The increase of 2 points in the gap has contributed to the growth of population. In Kerala not only both the rates are alongwith the gap between the two rates are at lowest level.

The mother nature has its own fight back mechanism. When its carrying capacity exceeds, the nature with this mechanism made the large sized animals like dinosaures completre extinct. The human race has already crossed the carrying capacity of the nature. Before the nature uses its fight back mechanism, we the human race, should do some thing positive to save ourselves, through stabilisation of PGR. The human race, intelligent among all the creatures on earth is solely responsible for the present situation, with our intelligence we only can make this earth a beautiful place to live in.

The CDR which was 27 during 1951, came down to 9 (2001). This reduction was possible not by any law but by awareness of the human beings. This awareness is not seen in other aspects as in the birth rate. People are still waiting for the male child and contribute for population growth.

Lat us, the thinkers aware of the possible danger of the human balloon and make the fellow human being aware of the same. Once this awareness is created, the principle of "Necessity is the mother of invention" automatically works out. These are more than 15 Acts in connection with the population control measures. But they showed little significant improvement. For instance, the government have been implementing a number of family planning, welfare measures since 1951 by providing cash incentives, green cards, etc. But the benefits of the measures could only be availed by urban population. The rural population, consisting of 85 per cent, it appears not aware of such schemes. Those who are aware also do not reap the benefits because of social customs, religious superstition etc. Further these programmes are target oriented, as such the executors, are forced to show higher figures of achievement than the actual ones to avoid explanation to the authorities.

The human race, like that of a balloon is going to burst at any moment and the entire human race may extinct if the human awareness is not created which in term solve the problems that are associated with the growth of population.

Suggestions

(1) To achieve the stability in the population growth following measures are suggested.

(i) Let us aware ourselves and make our fellow human beings aware of the alarming, growth of population. This can be achieved by providing compulsory education to all in 6-14 age group.

(ii) As an educated mother can create awareness in the entire family, female education—should be given high priority and made compulsory.

(iii) School and college curricular should include a chapter on population growth explaining the gravity of the situation and the problems associated with it.

(iv) The women, in rural area should encourage to form more and more self-help groups (SHG). The educated women groups should create awareness among them by formal and internal meetings, discussions to have small family and discourage waiting for male child and scanning and female foetitide.

(v) The government and non-government agencies should organise different entertainment programmes through dramas, TV shows, highlighting the advantages of small family and evil effects of abnormal growth of population alongwith the problems associated with it.

(vi) The target oriented approach of family planning schemes and cash incentives, green cards be discontinued. The executors of such schemes need not concentrate on achieving targets and show higher figures of achievement. Rather they can concentrate on the schemes instead of unnecessary paper work.

(vii) Frequent meetings, seminars, conferences, be held (in both Urban and Rural areas) to enlighten the public in general and rural mass in particular about the need of stabilising the PGR. These should be held by giving less priority to pomp and show.

((viii) The P.R. Act (Peoples Representation Act) be suitably amended so as to deprive persons, having more than 2 children to contest in elections to Parliament, Assembly, Panchayats, similarly such person should not be given any higher posts of office.

(ix) Finally strict control should be exercised on the publishers, writers of provocative pornography literature and media should also cooperate in not tele -casting such provocative and sex oxiented programmes and movies.

With the implementation of these measures, it is possible to create human awareness which automatically help maintaining the Population growth in limits.

References

Census Reports of India 1951 onwards.

Cempetition Success Review, May, 2001

Yojana, Vol.43, No. 12, Dec., 1999 — Demographic Transactions in South—Sahay K.B.

Competition Affairs, March, 2001 Issue No. III, Vol. XIV.

New Indian Express (English daily) dt. Mar. 28, April, 12, 2001.

Samaj (Oriya Daily) date: Feb. 26, March- 8, 13, 15, 16, 22, 26, 29, 31. April- 6, 11, 13, 20, and 27. 2001.

Dharitri (Oriya daily) dt. April 15, 2001.

Anupam Bharata (Oriya daily) dt. March, 28, 2001.

12

Population Issues and Challenges

—Prakash Ch. Misra

As we are in 21st century. This is the right time to look back and have an appraisal of the last century's development. So that we can know where we have arrived after a century? And where does our human society stand at the turn of the century? No doubt this turning point provides an opportunity to introspect, to take stock of our efforts to know where we have flourished and where we have floundered. Basing on this we can look forward to and can forsee the challenges of the 21st century.

The country has made admirable strides in various sectors during century. But it is also equally true that we have lagged behind in certain areas in comparison to our neighbours. Those are the problem areas which needs nation's priorities. One of such area which we must certainly address ourselves is the problem of growing population. Nothing disturbs us as much as the phenomenal rate at which our population is growing. Every year we add to our population as many people as live in Australia. It means that whatever wealth or goods or facilities we generate every year has to be shared by about 15 million more people which in turn, lowers our growth rate. Our schools, colleges, hospitals, transport systems etc even today are very inadequate.

Nevertheless, it is a matter of shame that 50 years after independence, 170 millions suffer from hunger, 48 per cent of our population (482 million) continue to be illiterate, maternal, infant and child mortality figures are alarmingly high, the majority of our villages have no roads, not even access to a basic necessity like drinking water. With only 2.5 per cent of the world's land area, we have to support as much as 16 per cent (860 millions) of the world's population, on merely 1.5 per cent of the world's income! This highlights the stark truth that without definite success in population control, the full benefits of our progress will continue to elude us. If only all of us could have taken this fundamental problem more seriously, our economy would not have reached the low ebb it did a few years ago.

Forget future benefits for the moment. We face that stark reality today of millions unemployed and 30 per cent having insufficient income to support themselves. Law and order enforcing agencies, the public services are stretched to breaking point.

A related danger is that because of our concentration on economic development, necessary as it is, not enough funds are left for health and education. We cannot allow welfare to be traded for economic growth.

Present Position

India's population has crossed 1 billion mark by May 11,2000. This is according to information of the Ministry of Health and Family Welfare, although according to UN estimates this incident had happened by mid August, 1999.

India's population was 347 million at the time of Independence (1947), which very rapidly rose to 850 million by 1990, and crossed the billion mark by mid-May, 2000. Thus, a population bomb is fast ticking to explode to a very fearful 1.65 billion in the year 2050—when it will surpass even China's population. By then, India will have the most dubious distinction of being the world's most populous country; but without much prosperity and having almost half of her population living below the poverty line. In 1997, 37 per cent of population or 360 million population was below the poverty line, and their numbers will greatly swell in future.

India's population has grown 4 times between 1901 and 2000, and almost tripled since 1941. This is mainly due to rapid decline in mortality, which was not accompanied by similar fast decline in fertility levels. So the key to population control lies actually in ensuring rapid fertility control. At present, India's population is growing by 15.33 million per year. This involves an addition of 43000 new babies daily, or 1 birth per 2 seconds. Right now, in India, 2 lakh villages (30 per cent of all villages) do not have clean drinking water, and 75-80 per cent of rural population do not have sanitary facilities; 25-40 per cent do not have adequate housing; and more than 30 per cent are denied modem health service. Even primary schools are absent in one third of the total villages in India Denial of such basic amenities of life will further aggravate when these will be added by further population explosion.

Such spurt in population will further aggravate socio-economic impact on economic development, resource utilization, and environmental degradation. Massive social overhead costs will be involved to provide basic needs of increasingly swelling population like, food, clothing, shelter, education, employment, transport, health services, and to maintain minimum standard of quality of life. Such a huge burden on the economy of the country will further cripple its economic growth and development; and severely limits its scope for prosperity, and its future. Increasing unemployment, and lack of savings and investment will aggravate the crucial problems of poverty in India.

State's Picture

There is considerable state-wise variations in demographic and socio-economic conditions. Population growth and fertility rates are much less where literacy and education are on higher levels, like Kerala, Goa, Mizoram, etc. Conversely, fertility levels and population growth rates are at very high levels where widespread female illiteracy and rampant poverty are persisting, like in UP, MP, Bihar, Rajasthan. Considerable differences also exist in rural and urban part of each state.

So, it is wise now to visualise rural-urban differences, and to assess state-wise variations in such situations. For such assessment, a factor analysis is performed on all the main variables of rural and urban part of all states, which has generated two main factors, with a given value exceeding greater than 1.0 explaining 81.6 per cent of total variance. These two dimensions are identified as follows:

1. "High-female illiteracy, poverty, high TFR, high IMR, and little availability of health services" dimension (explaining 71.8 per cent of variance).
2. "Prosperity, low TFR, low IMR, more health services and more contraceptive use" dimension (explains another 9.8 per cent)

It is indeed extremely remarkable that these two factors have been very successful to capture essence of socio-economic demographic-cum-policy structure of the present-day India: that is, depicting that 72 per cent of Indian's suffer, both socially and spatially, from acute illiteracy, poverty, high TFR, and IMR, and a complete lack of health services, in the one hand, and about 10 per cent of people and regions some what enjoy the privilege of prosperity, good health services, contraceptive, sterilizations, antenaial care, child immunization and so forth, and consequently, manifest a low, TFR and low IMR, on the other hand. Indeed, this picture correctly manifests India at present.

According to different state's relative position or relative picture on this multidimentional space, the following four main clusters are found out.

1. Cluster 1: Out of 37 regions of India, thus studied, only 12 are much developed regions, developed on all the three dimensions (D, S, P,), demographically, socio-economically, and health-wise, (Cluster 1). These regions/states are: Kerala (Urban), Kerala (Rural), Goa (U), Goa, (R), Maharastra (U), Gujarat (U), Punjab (Urban), Andhra Pradesh (U), Himachal Pradesh (U), Delhi (U), Jammu-Kashmir (U), and Rajasthan (U).
2. Cluster 2: Another 9 are on the incipient demographic transition and may show some substantial improvement in the next 5 and 10 years (Cluster 2). They include: Haryana (U), West Bengal (U). Tamil Nadu (U), Madhya Pradesh (U), Assam (U). Uttar Pradesh (U), Bihar (U), Rajasthan (U), and Orissa (U). They are just on the threshold of development.
3. Cluster 3: On the otherhand, there still exist about 8 underdeveloped regions Tamil Nadu (Rural), Gujarat (Rural), Haryana (R), Maharastra (R), Himachal Pradesh (R), Andhra Pradesh (R) , Jammu-

Kashmir (R) and Punjab (R) which show much female illiteracy, widespread poverty, moderately high TFR, moderately high IMR, and only slight health services and family planning practices. These states and regions need considerable revamping of their health services as well as sincere and sustained efforts for poverty alleviation.

4. Cluster 4: Finally, the hardcore areas of severe underdevelopment regions lie in such areas: Uttar Pradesh (Rural), Bihar (Rural), Madhya Pradesh (Rural), Rajasthan (Rural), Karnataka (Rural), and Assam (Rural). These regions suffer from very high female illiteracy, widespread poverty, high TFR, high IMR, little health services, and little family planning practices. Very large and highly populous states, they need very urgent action-oriented programmes for demographic transition and employment generation. These hitherto neglected and marginalized regions must be given the topmost attention for economic regeneration and demographic decline.

To sum up, in the context of population planning, as we enter the 21st century, one envisage the following five major challenges for India:

1. Rapid urban growth and the virtual collapse of the urban infrastructure in all our cities and towns;
2. Worsening social environment leading to conflict and violence;
3. Threat to political stability arising out of growing demographic and economic imbalance;
4. The unholy combination of tradition and technology, leading to gender disparity and its adverse impact

on the female foetus and the girl child in particular and also the overall status of women; and

5. The rise of religious fundamentalism and its adverse impact on the family planning programme.

We need bold steps and high calibre leadership to meet these challenges.

Population growth	*From*	*To*	*Period taken*
1st billion 1-2 billion	1830	1930	1 century
2nd billion 2-3 billion	1930	1960	30yrs
3rd billion 3-4 billion	I960	1975	15yrs
4th billion 4-5 billion	1975	1987	12yrs
5th billion 5-6 billion	1987	1997	10yrs

Table Growth and Distribution of Population in the Major Regions 1750-2050

Major Regions	1750	1800	1850	1900	1950	1999	2025	2050
World total	791	978	1262	1650	2524	5768	8039	2367
Africa	106	107	111	133	224	771	1290	2026
Asia	502	635	809	947	1402	3637	1785	5443
Europe	163	203	276	408	547	728	701	638
Latin America and Caribbean	16	24	38	74	166	512	690	810
North America	2	7	26	82	172	303	369	384
Oceania	2	2	2	6	13	30	41	45

Total Fertility Rate (TFR), 1998-99 TFR-15-49 Years

Sl. No	*States*	*Urban*	*Rural*	*Total*
1.	Uttar Pradesh	2.88	4.31	3.99
2.	Rajasthan	2.98	4.06	3.78
3.	Bihar	2.75	3.58	3.48
4.	Madhya Pradesh	2.61	3.56	3.31
5.	Haryana	2.25	3.13	2.88
6.	Gujarat	2.33	3.01	2.71
7.	Maharashtra	2.24	2.74	2.52
8.	Orissa	2.19	2.50	2.46
9.	Assam	1.50	2.39	2.31
10.	West Bengal	1.69	2.49	2.29
11.	Andhra Pradesh	2.07	2.32	2.25
12.	Punjab	1.79	2.42	2.21
13.	Tamil Nadu	2.12	2.22	2.18
14.	Himachal Pradesh	1.74	2.18	2.14
15.	Karnataka	1.89	2.25	2.13
16.	Kerala	1.51	2.07	1.96

Source: Compiled from preliminary reports of NFHS—2, 2000 (*International Institute for Population Sciences, Bombay,* 2000)

Country	*Average Annual Population growth (%)*			*Total Fertility Rate*			*% of births of women aged*		*IMR per 1000 in primary*	
	1970-80	*1980-93*	*1993-2000*	*1970-80*	*1980-93*	*1993-2000*	*<20*	*>3*	*1970*	*1990*
India	2.2	2.0	1.8	5.5	3.7	3.2	12	10	137	80
China	1.8	1.4	0.9	5.8	2.0	1.9	4	5	69	30
Thailand	2.7	1.7	0.9	5.5	2.1	2.1	7	10	73	36
Malaysia	2.4	2.5	2.3	5.5	3.5	3.0	7	14	45	13
South Korea	1.8	1.1	0.9	4.3	1.7	1.8	2	10	46	11

Source: Human Development Report 1995 and World Development Report 1995.

Birth, Death and Natural Growth Rate in Major States, 1998 (per thousand population)

Sl No.	*Birth Rate Rank India/States*	*Birth Rate*	*Death Rate*	*Natural Growth Rate*	*Growth Rate Rank*
1.	India	26.4	9.0	17.4	
2.	Uttar Pradesh	32.4	10.5	21.9	2
3.	Rajasthan	31.5	8.8	22.7	1
4.	Bihar	31.1	9.4	21.7	3
5.	Madhya Pradesh	30.6	11.2	19.4	5
6.	Assam	27.7	10.1	17.6	6
7.	Haryana	27.6	8.1	19.5	4
8.	Orissa	25.7	11.1	14.6	11
9.	Gujarat	25.3.	7.8	17.5	7
10.	Himachal Pradesh	22.5	7.7	14.8	8
11.	Punjab	22.4	7.7	14.7	9
12.	Maharashtra	22.3	7.6	14.7	10
13.	Andhra Pradesh	22.3	8.8	13.5	14
14.	Karnataka	22.0	7.9	14.1	12
15.	West Bengal	21.3	7.5	13.8	13
16.	Tamil Nadu	18.9	8.4	10.5	16
17.	Kerala	18.2	6.4	11.8	15

Source: Registrar General, India, SRS Bulletin, Oct.-99

References

Anita, F.P. Should our population be alloyed to explode', *Forum of Free Enterprise* (FFE), Bombay, 14th Sept. 1989.

S.P. Godrej, *Population Development and Environment* FFE. 15th Dec. 1994.

L.P. Singh, "Population growth vis-a-vis Human Resources Development in India," *Employment News*, Aug. 1998.

Sekhar Mukherji, Syndrome of proverty and population explosion in India—*Yojana,* Sept. 2000, vol. 44, No. 9.

Lalit Panicker, Census 2001: Its about people not population—a special report, *Times of India,* Feb. 2001.

Ashis Bose, Population Stabilisation in India: Progress and pitfals *Employment News*, New Delhi, Aug. 2000.

Girish Chandra, National Population Policy 2000: New policy seeks stable population by 2045. *Yojana*, vol. 44.

Abbreviations

IMR	Infant Mortality Rate
TFR	Total Fertility Rate
NFHS	National Family Health Survey
SRS	Simple Random Survey
NPP	National Population Policy
NRR	Net Reproductive Rate

13
Population vs. Economic Development

—Roopesh Kumar Misra

Amidst the various problems our country is undergoing currently population problem is crucial one. The alarming increase of population creates a great threat to the economic development of the country. India alone has more than 100 crore of people next to China. India like other developing countries has more pressure on population.

Population Growth

As per the census of 1991, the population of India was 846.3 million which was 683.32 million during the census 1981. This shows an increase of 163 million from 1981 to 1991. This addition is more than the total population of Japan. India has 2.4 per cent of total world land area harbouring 16 per cent of world population. The progressive growth rate over 1901 reveals an explosive situation during the years to come. The population trend of India during the period from 1901 to 2001 is explained in the Table 1.

From the table 1 it reveals that the population in 1921 was on negative. But after 1921, it was noticed a tremendous growth rate of population. The percentage of annual growth

Table 1

Population of India from 1901 to 2001

Year	*Population (Million)*	*Decadal absolute*	*Growth per cent*	*Annual exponential rate per cent*	*Progressive Growth rate (per cent)*
1901	238.39	-	-	-	-
1911	252.09	13.70	5.75	0.56	5.75
1921	251.32	0.77	0.31	0.03	5.43
1931	278.97	27.65	11.80	1.04	17.02
1941	318.66	39.69	14.22	1.33	33.65
1951	361.08	47.42	13.31	1.25	51.47
1961	439.23	78.15	21.51	1.96	84.25
1971	548.15	108.92	24.80	2.20	129.99
1981	683.32	135.17	24.66	2.22	186.64
1991	864.30	162.98	23.50	2.11	254.00
2001	1027.00	180.63	21.34	-	-

Source: Government of India Economic Survey Census Reports.

rate is increasing but in 1991 it has decreased only 14 per cent. According to world population report India will have a population of 1393.9 million by the year 2025. During the year 1990-95 the birth rate of the country was 29 per thousand and death rate was 10 persons per thousand.

Need of Population Control

Alarming increase of population has badly effects the growth and development of the country. It creates various social, economic and political problems in the developing nations like ours. The basic problems like, food, clothing unemployment, health, housing, drinking water, education communication are badly affected due to increase of population rapidly. It is also arresting the rise in per capita income of the country and affecting adversely on the capital formation as well as causing shortage of essential goods and services. To decrease the rapid growth of population, Government, social organisation and public irrespective of caste, colour, sex and religion should take some positive steps to curtail the growth rate to a sizeable extent.

These are discussed below:

India in World Population

The population of India in world in selected countries is explained in the Table 2.

Table 2

India in World Population in Selected Countries

Sl No.	*Name of the Country*	*Population in Percentage*
1.	China	21.03
2.	India	16.87
3.	USA	4.63
4.	Indonesia	3.49
5.	Brazil	2.80
6.	Pakistan	2.58
7.	Russian Fed.	2.42
8.	Bangladesh	2.13
9.	Japan	2.09
10.	Nigeria	1.84
11.	Other Countries	40.12
	Total	100

Source: Cęnsus of India—2001, Director of Census Operation, Orissa, p. 14.

From the table it reveals that the 10 countries mentioned in the table occupy 60 per cent of World's population and rest 40 per cent. China and India occupies nearly (37.90 per cent) 38 per cent of world's population. Unless a positive check is to be taken on the growth rate of the population it will blast at any time and will cause uncontrolled problems.

Measure to Lower Birth Rate

The ever increasing birth rate is creating problems in the society. At present the population growth is 15.33 million per year in India. A new mouth comes to our country at two seconds interval. So per day nearly 43,000 new babies are born in India. Steps to be taken to lower the birth rate. For this purpose an active educational campaign be there mostly in the rural areas. Non-Government organisations should come forward to educate the rural masses regarding the need of family planning for the development of the country. The concept of male child is one of the reasons for growth rate of population. Still, the people are in opinion that they should have one male child and one waiting even after three to four girl children. The slogan like "We need one child—whether boy or girl". Poverty, also taken into consideration to increase the birth rate. It is found that the birth rates are high in underdeveloped and in developing countries in comparison to developed nations. The poverty ratio of India during the year is 27.09 in rural and 23.62 in urban area. Orissa is top in the list. That is 47.15, 42.60 in Bihar.

Woman Education

Literacy is one of the good indicator of development of a society. It provides an important source for information for implementation of policies and programmes by the central Government and State Governments of the country. The literacy rate in India from 1951 is explained in the Table 3.

Table 3

Literacy Rate of Males and Females (in Percentage)

Sl. No.	*Census Years*	*Persons*	*Male*	*Females*
1.	1951	18.33	27.16	8.86
2.	1961	28.30	40.40	15.35
3.	1971	34.45	45.96	21.97
4.	1981	43.57	56.38	29.76
5.	1991	52.21	64.13	39.29
6.	2001	65.38	75.85	54.16

Source: Director of Census Operation, Orissa, p. 78 Census of India, 2001.

From the table it shows that the literacy rate of India is not upto the mark comparisan to other countries of the world. The literacy is very less in comparisan to literacy rate of male. Unless the females are educated the plans and policies implemented to check the population will be no use. The females must be aware of the evils causes of population growth and specially on male child. If this literacy rate will continue the population growth of the country can not be reduced.

Social Activities and Employment of Women

If the women are engaged in social activities and provided some employment opportunities the birth rate may be decreased to some extent. The political scenario of women in some different countries are explained in the Table 4.

From the table it is obvious that the political interference of women in the world is very negligible. Unless they should come forward or educated or given social status in every walk of the society the population can not decline.

Table 4

Political Senario of Women in World

Year	*Happening*
1918	In England women got their voting power.
1920	In America the women got their voting power.
1971	The women of Switzerland got their voting right.
2001	Women of eight countries are still to voting right.
2001	No lady parliamentarian in 14 countries.
2001	Out of 200 countries of world 48 countries have no lady minister.

Source: Samaj Dated 08.03.2001.

Experience shows that education, employment and social status of women will bring a decline trend in birth rate. Education and employment of women will also raise their social status. Late marriage, abstinence in martial relation and use of contraceptives can play a very useful role in restricting the birth rate. An initiative towards avoidance of birth has been the liberalisation of Abortion. Under the Termination of Pregnancies Act 1971, abortion is not allowed in all cases where it is not likely to have an adverse effect on the health of the prospective mother.

Family Welfare Programme

The family welfare programme is to educate the eligible couples to use different methods for limiting the family size and promote responsibility in parenthood. To promote family welfare programmes are conducted at different hospitals, Sub-Centres, Primary Health Centres, Community health centres, Post-Partum centres, and voluntary organisations are involved in the programme to reduce birth rate. During the sixth plan period an atmosphere was created by the Government of India to adopt different family planning techniques to reduce the birth rate. The success of the family planning programme depends on the involvement of people. For this persuasion is necessary to educate the people to adopt small family norm. Special programmes like—information, education and Communication (IEC) should be taken to remove the birth against girl child. The concept of "One family one child" to undertake by the Government and non-government organisations by educating the couple. The Government of India should take bold step to disable a person to contest for MLA and MP if he/she has more than two children. A committee of NDC (National Development Council) on population was constituted in February 1992 to consider various issues like family literacy, age for marriage (both girls and boys), employment opportunities for women etc. to reduce birth rate. The Government has also taken a step in 1994 to introduce family planning programme in Panchayat Raj to reduce birth rate or to educate the people at grass root level.

Conclusion

Programmes undertaken by the Government of India, state governments and Non-government organisations will be of no use unless the people of the country will accept it. The willingness with enthusiasm to participate in the movement to reduce the birth rate for the development of the Nation by the people and mostly by the rural people all our plans and programmes will not come to success as per our desire. So the movement must be started by the people itself, otherwise all programmes will not be a success to the desired extent. The government machinaries should be very honest in implementing the plans and there should not be any distinction between people to people.

References

Census of India, 2001.

Employment News—March, 2001.

Economic Survey—Govt. of Orissa, Bhubaneswar.

Yojana—New-Delhi-Sept., 2000.

14
Growth of Population and Social Infrastructure

—Premananda Pradhan

Almost fifty five years ago at the time of Independence of India the total population of the entire subcontinent was about 33 crore. Now India alone has more than 100 crore of people. China is the most populous country in the world with its vast area nearly three times the geographical size of India. India's population crossed the one billion mark in the year 2000. It is expected that India will overtake China as the most populous nation in the world some time between 2050-2075 A.D.

The boom of population explosion is expanding day-by-day. The following statistical table (Table 1) shows the growth rate of population of India.

From the following statistics, it is evident that the population growth till 1921 was very small even negligible. But after 1921 there has been an alarming growth rate of population. During 1981 census, there was 68.52 crores. It has increased to 84 crores during 1991 and has crossed to 100 crores at the close of the 20th century.

Increasing population has varying impact on economy amongst which the problem of social infrastructure is by far the most important problem. Social infrasturcture, refers to the expansion and development of housing, education, drinking water facilities, health status, road-transport, communication and postal services.

Table 1

Growth of Population in India

Census Year	*Population in lakhs*	*Decemal increase or decrease in Lakhs*	*Percentage increase or decrease during the decade*	*Annual Growth rate (%)*
1901	2384	-	-	-
1911	2521	+137	+5.75	6.56
1921	2513	-8	-6.30	(-) 0.03
1931	2790	+277	+11.00	1.06
1941	3187	+397	+14.23	1.34
1951	3611	+424	+13.31	1.26
1961	4392	+781	+21.64	1.93
1971	5482	+1090	+24.80	2.24
1981	6852	+1370	+25.00	2.28
1991	8463	+1611	+23.50	2.14
2001	10270	-	-	-

Source: Census Reports.

Needless to mention that excessive growth of population has created various problems which are manifested in social, political economical and environmental scenarios. Let us have a glance impact of population on social infrastructure.

Problem of Education and Health

Rapidly rising population increases the number of children in the School going age and "also arises the enrolment of students in College and University education.

This is a type of situation we are facing in India, expenditure on education is an investment in men for raising the productivity of labour force but inbetween there is a huge time lag. In 1981 total population in the age group of 6-14 years was one fifty six (156) million and the expenditure per pupil. Being Rs. 144/- per year, increase in expenditure on education can be estimated at Rs.246 crores per year, in addition to this if we add the increasing burden of University education then this increasing burden of expenditure would be much higher.

Moreover, this rising population in India is also increasing the burden of enhanced expenditure on medical care, public health and housing accommodation. The population explosion, coupled with a lack of proper health services has brought the country to the verge of a loosing bottle against various diseases like malaria and tuberculosis. Professor Cax Yasudin of the Tata Institute of Social Sciences said that about 8 thousand people in the age group of 35 to 45 years die, every year due to tuberculosis in metro cities.

Problem of Housing

The number of absolutely homeless households were 6 million in 1981 as estimated. About 51.2 million persons living in slums and have occupied public land without permission. About 50 per cent of the urban households are living in one room dwelling place. It is estimated that the total shortage of housing units as 23.3 million in 1981 which would go up to 41 million units by 2000 A.D. The housing shortage in the country has been estimated 31 million units in 1990-91, where shortage in rural areas are 10.4 million units. So, the problem of shelter is growing day-by-day.

No doubt, the problem of housing is general. However, it has become more acute for those who are in the grip of poverty. According to the 12 th report of the National Sample Survey, about 73 per cent of the households live in Kutcha structures having plinth and wall made up of non-durable materials like mud and roofs are built of grass and leaves. The majority of dwelling places lack basic amenities such as sanitary, waste disposal, ventilation, lighting, drinking water etc.

City Transport Services

Over growing population has aggravated the problem of city transport services. As it is observed that the number of buses, trackers are increasing day-by-day, there are overcrowding in city-transport services. People quarrel for seat purposes. The Indian Railway system is the largest network in the world. Still there is problem of railway transport.

Drinking Water

The main requirements for public health protection are adequate sanitary conditions and safe and sufficient drinking water. However, due to alarming growth of population, this provision has become still a distant dream. Bathing of men and animals are common in a particular pond. The same water is used for drinking water purposes. In India, water borne diseases such as gastroenterities, diarrhoea, dysentery, cholera etc. are due to the present of bacteria in drinking water. The global burden of main disease and death from the microbial contamination of our environment is given in Table 2.

It has been further, cleared that, to protect the teeming millions from the water borne diseases Government of India is pending crores of money through (i) National Malaria Control programme (1958), National AIDS Control

Programme (1987), B.C.O. Vaccination Programme (1951) , Universal Immunisation Programme (1985) etc.

Table 2

Magnitude of Deaths by Diseases

Disease	*Case of disease*	*Death*
Cholera	3,84,000	11,000
Typhoid	5,00,000	25,000
Diarrhoea Disease	4,002,00,000	31,15,000

Table 3

Declining Sex Ratio

Year	*Sex ratio (No. of females 1000 males)*
1971	930
1981	934
1991	927
2001	933

Source: Census Report.

It has been revealed that population is the central problem which all other problems are revolving it. Therefore, population explosion must be controlled. In order to tackle the situation, the following measures may be forwarded:

1. Optimum utilisation of Mass Media, especially T.V. and Radio networks for motivation of the people has to be made.
2. Efforts should be made to raise the level of literacy among the poeple, particularly among women.
3. Present age of marriage may be raised through legislation.

4. Finally, intensive research in the methods and techniques of birth control must be made.

The sex-ratio (females per every 1000 males) in India has been adverse to women. It was 972 in 1901, declined to 941 in 1961, and was only 927 in 1991. It has reached at 933 for 2001.

The adverse sex ratio is due to low expectation of life at birth for females in the past compared to males. Highly discriminators socio-economic practices against the girl child has led to the declining sex-ratio. This declining sex ratio has determental effect on different realm of society. There is increasing trend of violence against women, manifested in the form of rape, sexually assault, eve-teasing etc. Social crimes have increased a lot, leading to adverse impact on socio-economic lifes of people.

References

Employment News, "Population on 21st Century".

P. K. Dhar, *Indian Economy and its growing dimension*.

Mishra & Puri, *Indian Economy*.

K.P.M. & Sundaram Rudradatta, *Indian Economy*.

Mohinder, "Housing for rural poor, problem policies and prospectives." *Kurukshetra*, July 1999, p. 29.

Drinking Water Supply to Villages"—*Kurukshetra*, July, 1999, pp. 4 & 5.

15

Impact of Urbanisation on Environment

— S.N. Tripathy

Urbanisation refers to the process of population concentration entailing an increase in population living in urban areas. Urbanisation is a world-wide process and has been considered not only as an index of economic development but also as an important factor of social change. Urbanisation implies the re-distribution of population and a change in the demographic balance between rural and urban area. Natural increase of urban population and net-migration from the rural to urban areas are two important factors which can be attributed to the increase of urban population.

Trend of Urbanisation

India has 25.72 per cent of urban population constituting 217.2 million as per 1991 census. The magnitude and absolute size of urban population, however, is much larger than the total population of any country in the world except China and the U.S.A.

The 1981-91 decadal increase of 57.7 million in the urban population itself is much greater than the total population of most countries of Africa, Latin America and Europe.

Table 1

The Trend of Urbanisation in India

Census year	*No. of Urban areas/towns*	*Urban Population*	*Percentage of Urban Population to total Population*
1971	2590	109.1	19.91
1981	3378	159.5	23.34
1991	3768	217.2	25.72

Source: Census of India, Provisional Population Totals: Rural Urban Distribution, Paper No. 2 of 1991 New Delhi.

The Table 1 shows that the proportion of Urban Population of India was 19.91 per cent in 1971 census which increased to 23.34 per cent in 1981. Again in 1991, the total size of Urban Population in India increased to 217.2 million as compared to that of 159.5 million in 1981. In percentage terms, the growth of population was from 23.34 per cent to 25.72 per cent in 1991. Moreover, the total number of towns in India which were 2590 in 1971 gradually increased to 3378 in 1981 and to 3768 in 1991.

The thickly populated cities termed as mega cities with a population over 5 million as per 1991 census present one-third of the total Urban Population. The census data for 1991 clearly demonstrate the mega cities' population of Bombay, Calcutta, Delhi and Madras which stands at 12.57 million, 10.86 million, 8.58 million and 5.36 million respectively. Table 2 reveals the growth of Urban Population of these four mega cities which have been sharply increasing over the decades.

It is interesting to note that during 1981 census, Calcutta with 91.6 lakhs had the highest urban Population in India. But in 1991 Greater Bombay, occupied the top position in the list of highly urbanised populated mega cities with 125.7 lakhs of urban population.

Table 2
Population of Mega cities in the Population of 5 million and above (Population in lakhs)

Mega Cities	*1971*	*1981*	*1991*
Greater Bombay	59.7	82.3	125.7
Calcutta	70.3	91.6	108.6
Delhi	36.5	67.1	85.8
Madras	31.7	42.8	53.6

Source: Census of India.

Urbanisation is considerably accelerated by rural-urban migration. Factors like heavy indebtedness at disproportionate interest rates incurred for social functions, cronic drought situation, erosion of traditional crafts and profession as a result of competition from the modern sector, and many other complex factors are inter-woven in the fabric of rural-urban migration. As a result of migration and increasing trend of urbanisation, several environmental issues leads to air, water and noise pollution, sewage and drainage problems, slums and consequent climatic change. Unplanned urbanisation and rapid growth of cities cause congestion, increase in crime and pollution.

Slums

No Indian city today is free from the slums due to heavily exodus of population from the rural areas. The problem seems to be more serious in the mega cities. It is estimated, on an average, slum population constitute around 30 per cent of most of the urban cities in India. The growth of slums is essentially a problem of Urban poor where there is lack of high wage employment opportunities and also absence of decent shelter. The shelter problem in major Urban areas is manifested in the tremendous over crowding, proliferating slums, unauthorised colonies and inadequate access to basic services through slum dwellers, which form a part of the urban economy.

Slum dwellers are mostly poor and unskilled labourers who engage themselves in low-wage jobs in the informal sector. The city administration considers such a settlement as illegal and therefore, does not provide municipal services to them. The result is the inevitable growth of slums which provides a substandard living.

Environmental Pollution

Human problems are multiplied to a new dimension because of urbanisation, pollution, scarcity of non-renewable resources and deforestation. Urbanisation increases surface humidity, slowing of wind, evaporation, stimulation of rainfall and heat stress etc.

Noise pollution which means an undesirable and unpleasant sound caused by large number of motor vehicles on road, community noise, sound due to use of domestic appliances, electric machines etc.

Space pollution emerges because of over-crowding which has been associated with urbanisation. Due to deplorable environmental conditions, absence of sewage facilities, lack of provision of drinking water, lack of disposal facilities for the waste materials health hazards are created. The children of the poorer sections of the society are the worst victims as they suffer from diarrhoea, dysentery, typhoid due to adverse environment.

Impact on Land

Industrialisation in urban areas converts fertile agricultural land into non-agricultural use. Besides, conversion of large acres of green tracts within and around cities into residential, official and commercial establishments creates environmental imbalances. It limits the open space available per person. High demand for housing as a result of accelerated urbanisation, leads to encroachment of public areas, children's play ground, open parks.

About four million acres of rural land have been subsumed by cities in the last 40 years and another two million are expected to vanish by the year 2000. Some three million acres of top soil are needed to house the current urban population in brick structures but atleast twice that amount is being washed away each year.

Industrial pollution is wide-spread. Fertilizer, paper, sugar, steel plant, pesticide units, refineries—all these industries have polluted the rivers, land and atmosphere.

Family and Social Values

The institution of family is adversely affected due to urbanisation. In the process of urbanisation, the joint family system has broken yielding pace for nuclear types of family. People are compelled to leave their family, old and dependent parents behind while they come to the urban areas in search of employment and livelihood.

Urbanisation has the detrimental affect on moral values. The magnitude of crimes in urban areas are much higher than in rural areas. Unemployment among educated youths, drug addiction, neglect of parents and their inability to spare more time for their children etc., are the vital causes of crimes.

Policy Options

In view of the foregoing discussion, it is imperative to suggest policy options for ensuring healthy environmental conditions.

The municipality and local bodies need to be financially sound to take up varied activities to counter environmental issues.

The NGOs can play a crucial role by taking up small projects at micro level, to protect and improve the environment.

Since urbanisation inadvertently modifies the local climate and environment, by raising the temperature, this could be tackled by afforestation programme in the public places, parks and around the colonies etc.

Major environmental concerns for women are water and sanitation. Creation of awareness among women about the importance of clear drinking water and sanitation help in improving the immediate environment and health of urban people.

As regards air pollutions caused by motor vehicles, suitable designed vehicles may be introduced with the use of pollution-free fuels, introduction of smokeless cooking stoves, bio-gas burners, conservation of fuels could counter environmental hazards.

More emphasis should be given for development of rural industries especially the traditional crafts alongwith necessary technology so that self-employment opportunities can be expanded in rural set-up.

Improvement in slums as well as in the living condition of slum dwellers is needed to minimise the adverse impact of urbanisation.

References

S.N. Tripathy, (2000), *Rural Development*, Discovery Publishing House, New Delhi.

S.N. Tripathy, and Pande, Shankar (1999), *Fundamentals of Environmental Studies*, Vrinda Publications (P) Ltd. Delhi.

Index

❑❑❑